Helsinki

DAUGHTER OF THE BALTIC

MATTI KLINGE — LAURA KOLBE

Helsinki

DAUGHTER OF THE BALTIC

A SHORT BIOGRAPHY

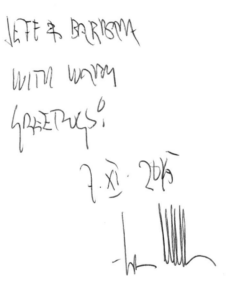

OTAVA PUBLISHING COMPANY LTD HELSINKI

The first printout of the revised edition

Matti Klinge has written the chapters covering
pages 7–32, 43–47, 62–72, 90–96,146–153
and Laura Kolbe those covering
pages 33–42, 48–61, 73–89, 97–145

Illustrations chosen by the authors
Translation by Malcolm Hicks
Jacket design by Tuukka Rantala

Printed by:
Otava Book Printing Ltd
Keuruu 2007

ISBN-13: 978-951-1-21813-5

CONTENTS

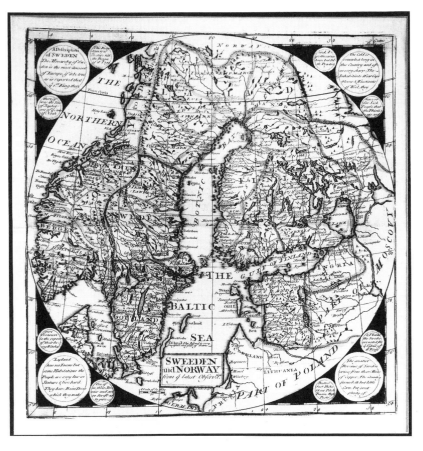

The history of Helsinki is closely connected with the commercial, military and political history of the Baltic Sea. Important cities have always existed in the southwestern corner of the Baltic, from Kalmar to Hamburg, and around the Gulf of Finland, from Novgorod and St. Petersburg to Vyborg, Tallinn and Helsinki.

GUARDIAN OF A VITAL NAVIGATION ROUTE

The foundation, growth and significance of the city of Helsinki may be said to be bound up with the whole status of the Baltic Sea, and particularly of the Gulf of Finland. This gulf is no more than a hundred kilometres wide at its broadest, and serves as a channel leading from the central Baltic to the River Neva, from where the route leads on to the great inland sea of Lake Ladoga and further into the interior of Russia. Helsinki itself is located on an ancient sea route, within the spheres of influence of strong commercial and military interests and at a point of conflict between them.

There have been significant commercial centres at the eastern and western ends of the Baltic Sea for over a thousand years – together with harbours and the fortresses needed to protect them. In the west were the merchants and pirates of the Frisian Islands and Rügen and the towns of Haithabu (Schleswig), Hamburg and Lübeck, and later those of Copenhagen and Helsingör. All of these towns provided connections between the North Sea and the Baltic Sea and routes up the rivers into the interior of Germany.

The major centre at the eastern end of the Baltic Sea was Novgorod, at the head of a host of smaller towns and fortresses on the channel leading to it. The Varangians, or Vikings, from the Baltic region had been a crucial element in the founding of the city of Novgorod and the old state of Russia in the 9th century, and the name *Vargskär* applied to the islands housing the fortress of Sveaborg, or Suomenlinna, off Helsinki, may well be derived from the Russian word for these people, *Varyag*. Other place names of the same kind are to be found on the routes frequented by the Varangians. From Lake Ladoga and Novgorod the connections continued into the great river systems of central Russia and on to the Volga and the Caspian Sea. From that point onwards two major trade routes existed, the Silk Road to Persia and China and a route through the Dnieper and Kiev to the Black Sea, Constantinople and the Mediterranean.

The state of Sweden consolidated itself in the 13th century and began to extend its influence eastwards, attempting in vain to overcome the Novogorodians at the Neva, approximately on the site of the present-day St. Petersburg, in 1240. The Swedes had built a castle at Vyborg by the end of that century, however, and achieved an eastern boundary under the Treaty of Pähkinäsaari in 1323 that bound the

western end of the Karelian Isthmus to the western religious and ju-
dicial traditions for a period that lasted until 1940/1944, even though
the national boundaries changed from time to time.

It was also during the 13th century that Denmark and Germany attempted to take advantage of the situation in the Baltic and the weak-
ness of Russia to establish their own bases in the region. Thus the
Germans created the city of Riga in 1201 and the Danes that of Reval,
or Tallinn, in 1219. Both shores of the Gulf of Finland gained pioneer
settlement in support of these new power structures, and both developed a military organization based on the existence of large land
holdings or estates.

Just as the name Tallinn reminds us of the city's Danish origins, the
name Helsinki and the boat symbol on the city's coat of arms remind
us of the Swedish settlers who came here from Helsingland. Some
of these inhabitants came during the period of systematic colonization in the 13th century, when the aim was to guarantee allegiance to
Sweden among the population of the coastal areas overlooking the
main navigation route to the east. The great figure behind the Swedish expansion eastwards was Earl Birger (Birger Jarl), who with this in
mind, and partly on the strength of the endeavour, consolidated Sweden as a state and founded a new capital for it, Stockholm.

In his doctoral thesis submitted to the Royal Turku Academy in
1754, the scholar Henrik Forsius of Helsinki provided an account of
the origins of his home town which was in keeping with the notion
of history accepted at that time:

It would be difficult and dangerous nowadays to say for certain at what period the Swedes
took possession over Uusimaa, as no definitively accurate − − documents have been handed
down to us on such events. Something close to the scientific truth may nevertheless be perceived in the claims of those who maintain that the new colony left its former dwelling
place during the reign of King Erik the Holy and travelled to their new lands under their
military leader Fale Bure. A number of chronicles − − of the heroic deeds of our fore-
fathers consistently indicate that an armed group from the provinces of Gestrikland and
Helsingland established themselves by force in this area of Uusimaa.

The boat on the coats of arms of both Uusimaa and Helsinki is a refer-
ence to this mythical history of the colonization of the area.

The name Helsinki applied at first to a church parish created in
the prosperous arable region about 20 km north of the modern city
centre, an area that is crossed by the River Vantaa (Vanda) on its way
from the interior region of Häme to the Gulf of Finland coast. This
area now lies in the borough of Vantaa and part of it is occupied by

8

the Helsinki-Vantaa International Airport. Travellers can in fact catch a glimpse of the old 14th century church on their way to the city centre. Like many other stone churches on the south coast of Finland, it provides a good reminder that the country has belonged to the Western European Christian cultural sphere from very early times.

The history of the Baltic region takes on a quite new aspect from around 1520 onwards. The Lutheran reformation and the tendency for tighter state organizations instead of principalities led to dissolution of the union between Denmark and Sweden, so that the latter, to which the present-day territory of Finland belonged, came to form a separate kingdom and developed into a centralized state on modern lines under King Gustavus I Vasa. Inspired by the doctrines of the Reformation, the king enhanced his own power by confiscating church property, and in 1540 a universal state taxation system was implemented that covered the whole country, replacing the old feudal structures. Two years later it was proclaimed that all the vast areas of unoccupied land in the country belonged to the crown. This marked the beginning of large-scale settlement of the land, especially in areas close to the eastern border.

King Gustavus I took it upon himself to found a major new commercial town beside the eastern trade route, to vie with the rich Hansa town of Tallinn, and was prepared to resort to the new means at the disposal of a centralized state in order to bring this about.

The history of Helsinki is said to have begun with the Royal Decree of 12th June 1550 ordering the merchants of the towns of Porvoo (Borgå), Tammisaari (Ekenäs), Rauma and Ulvila to move to a new town to be built beside the rapids on the River Vantaa in the parish of Helsinki. There had been talk in previous years of moving the city of Turku or of strengthening settlement at Vyborg by forcing merchants to move there, but the future Helsinki was better placed geographically to serve as a major trading centre located between east and west and destined to capture a large part of the trade then centred on Tallinn and other Baltic ports on the route between Russia and the North Sea and to provide a coastal outlet for trade with a substantial hinterland. The king was thus prepared to order the merchants to move several hundred kilometres in some cases in order to ensure a sufficiently powerful commercial base for this new town.

This decree provides evidence of the radical nature of Gustavus Vasa's reign in relation to the history of Sweden(-Finland) and the whole of the Baltic region. A loose Nordic union afflicted with internal strife was replaced in 1520 by a new kingdom of Sweden(-Finland), while Norway was correspondingly linked firmly with Den-

King Gustavus I Vasa, king of "the Sveas, Götas and Wends", who reigned from 1523 to 1560, disengaged Sweden from its union with Denmark-Norway and shaped it into a modern, centrally governed state. Part of this policy involved the conscious regulation of trade and the activities of the towns.

Perpetuò indigenæ Suecis rex regis habendi
Auctor GVSTAVVS, pectore maior, hic eſt.

mark. Thus developments in the Nordic region formed part of those common to most areas of Europe, giving rise to "modern" centralized principalities. At the same time a crisis also spread to the state maintained by the teutonic knights in the Baltic region and a long battle began over the division of this territory among Poland, Russia, Denmark and Sweden.

The former decentralized pattern of society was replaced by a fixed central organization which gradually eased power away from the church, the aristocracy and the cities and concentrated it in one central institution, the king. This in turn led, of course, to absolutism in the exercise of power, i.e. the exercise of supreme control by the king and his officials over the estates, corporations and regions, and over the church.

The aim of this modern centralized state was that its control should be extended to all aspects of society, including the founding and concentration of towns. When the New Testament was first translated into Swedish in 1526, it was necessary to explain to the people what was meant by "general taxation", but by the time a new Swedish translation and the first Finnish translation were published in the 1540's the people knew very well from experience what this implied. Gustavus I made the crown hereditary, superseding the old system under which the king was elected, and determinedly suppressed all attempts at rebellion. Finally, his son Charles IX in particular was responsible for the execution of a large proportion of the old aristocracy, not least those residing in Finland.

The long reign of King Gustavus I Vasa, from 1523 to 1560, guaranteed the success of the centralization process. It also meant the rise of a whole dynasty, in that his descendants reigned uninterrupted until 1818 (or 1809 in the case of Finland).

Sweden, Russia and Poland were at war almost throughout the latter half of the 16th century, in the Baltic region and in Karelia, by land and sea, and in addition there were the wars with Denmark. Once Tallinn had capitulated to the Swedes in 1561 and the rest of Estonia soon after, both shores or the Gulf of Finland in effect belonged to the Kingdom of Sweden.

This also meant, of course, that the whole point of founding the town of Helsinki to compete with Tallinn was lost. Helsinki grew into a substantial commercial town in the course of the century, and one or two fairly wealthy Dutch merchants established themselves there, but the state no longer attempted to promote its growth at the expense of other places or to afford it preferential treatment in any way.

A notable scholar from Helsinki, Sigfridus Aronus Forsius, published this little book on comets in 1618. Topelius wrote about Forsius on many occasions.

The whole trade with Russia suffered from the extended hostilities, and when the Treaty of Stolbova in 1617 finally marked the beginning of a long period of peace on this front, the border had moved a long way further east. Sweden at last had a town of its own on the River Neva, by the name of Nyen. On the other hand, Novgorod had lost much of its former glory to Moscow and the trade route across the Baltic was less important than in earlier times.

One of the early outstanding figures among the citizens of Helsinki, known as Helsingfors in Swedish and *Forsia* in Latin, was the scholar Sigfridus Aronus Forsius, who served in the course of his varied life as a schoolteacher in Tallinn, an army chaplain, an explorer on the Arctic Ocean coast and professor of Astronomy at the new University of Upsala before ending up as vicar of Tammisaari (Ekenäs). He died in 1624. Forsius became renowned for his learning, and also for his irregular living habits. He published an official almanac annually, containing predictions for the coming year, and left behind him a prodigious manuscript entitled *Physica*, which was an explanation of the origins of the world. This was eventually published only in the 1950's.

One significant event in the early history of Helsinki was the provincial assembly held in 1616, at which the young King Gustavus II Adolphus, grandson of Gustavus I, appealed to representatives of the four estates in the eastern part of his kingdom for support in the war against Russia and Poland. The older, legitimate branch of the Vasa dynasty, now ruling over Poland, had always had a faithful following in Finland, including the above-mentioned Forsius, but with the aid of Oxenstierna and others, Gustavus Adolphus succeeded in winning over the assembly, which acceded to his proposed war taxes and rejected the propaganda put about by King Sigismund.

When Sweden's position relative to Denmark and Russia had been consolidated through highly favourable treaties, the focal point of the war shifted to the Baltic region, where Livonia (the southern part of present-day Estonia and the northern part of Latvia) was transferred from Polish to Swedish control and subsequently, in 1630, to that of Germany. The participation of the King of Sweden(-Finland) and his troops in the Thirty Years' War meant the emergence of his country as a great power in Europe, and this in turn called for numerous structural and cultural reforms, including a complete reorganization of the administration and the promotion of education at the highest levels. The present University of Helsinki was founded in Turku in 1640. The reforms also included the raising of the status of the national capital, Stockholm, and the modernization of other towns. Practically all the towns in Sweden were replanned to give them a more regular, spaci-

It was the regency government of Queen Christina that decided to move Helsinki from the mouth of the River Vantaa to its present site on "Vironniemi", close to a better natural harbour. This took place in 1640, the same year when the Gymnasium in Turku was upgraded to a Royal University. This institution was later transferred to Helsinki. The picture is of the first Bible produced in Finnish, dating from 1642.

ous and impressive appearance. It was not possible to implement all the projects of this kind, but great changes were brought about in Helsinki, for example. The whole settlement was moved in 1640 from the Helsinki rapids (*Helsingfors*) at the mouth of the River Vantaa to the outer islands, close to the shipping channel that ran along the Gulf of Finland, to a place known of old by the name *Vironniemi, Estnäskatan*, which serves as a reminder of the original function of the area as a base for Estonian fishermen and traders.

The first history of Helsinki, written by Henricus Forsius, son of the vicar of the city, was published as a doctoral thesis in two folios at the Royal University of Finland in Turku in 1755 and 1757. The picture also shows part of the introductory lecture, with quotations from Cicero.

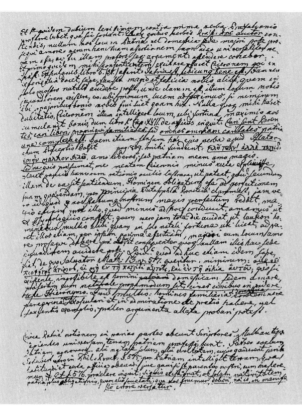

Both the Finnish University and the new town of Helsinki commemorate as their founder the child Queen Christina, daughter and heir of King Gustavus II Adolphus, the Minerva of the North.

The transfer of settlement to a position on the outer islands and adjacent to the main shipping route did not suffice to turn Helsinki into a significant city, however. On the contrary, its military position was more vulnerable than ever, and it was razed to the ground in 1713 in the course of the Great Northern War. War had broken out between Sweden and the newly strengthened Russia in 1700, and Russia had gained a decisive land victory at the battle of Poltava in 1709. Its subsequent maritime and coastal victories were then enacted in Finland and the Baltic region, with the conquest of Karelia, including Vyborg, and of Estonia and Livonia in 1710, the whole of Southern Finland as far as Turku in 1713, and Ostrobothnia the following year. The Russian

PRÆFATIO.

St, & semper fuit, omnibusque horis permanebit indubia veritas, quod domestica sede nulla nobis jucundior accidat; illam adolescentiæ palæstram quoties revisere, recognoscere, aut saltem memorando renovare nobis datum fuerit, juvenescere iterum & ad præteritos annos reverti nobis videamur. Mihi certe, cum per latè patentis philosophiæ campos eundo, argumentum expeterem, in quo elaborando quantillas ingenii mei vires experirer, patriæ pomœria terræ, *Helsingforsensis* in *Nylandia* urbis pristinam & hodiernam formam subjicere oculis, tam cum animo conjunctum, quam ab officio non alienum mihi visum fuit. Neque non illa me modo genuit, sed & erudiit; non proferendæ vitæ animali modo necessaria prospexit, sed & civili providere & præcavere, negotium suum esse voluit, ne per imperitiam ætatis in aliquam

A   vitæ

D. A. G.
SPECIMINIS ACADEMICI
DE

HELSING-FORSIA,

CELEBRI NYLANDIÆ EMPORIO,
PARS PRIOR,
QUAM,
Consensu ampl. Facult. Phil. in Regia academ.
ABOENSI,
PRÆSIDE
VIRO CL.
Mag. ALGOTHO A. SCARIN,
Histor. & philos. civ. PROF. Reg: & ord.
nec non academiæ BIBLIOTHECARIO,
Publicæ ventilationi modestè submittit,
HENRICUS FORSIUS,
HELSINGFORSIA·NYLANDUS,
In audit. superiori, ad d. VIII. Novembr. MDCCLV.
H. A. M. S.
ABOÆ, Imprerssit DIRECT. & Typogr. Reg. Magn. Duc.
Finland. JACOB MERCKELL.

Navy achieved its first large-scale victory off the peninsula of Hanko at the entrance to the Gulf of Finland. The Russians occupied Finland until the Treaty of Uusikaupunki (Nystad) was signed in 1721, at which point they returned the territory to Sweden with the exception of Karelia. During that war the Russians had a naval repair base on the islands that were later to become the fortress of Sveaborg (Suomenlinna).

Helsinki was rebuilt, and its third church, still a wooden one, was named after Queen Ulrika Eleonora, sister and heir to Charles XII. The name Ulrika, or Ulla, lives on in the names of streets and districts in Helsinki to remind us of the great fortress once planned for the southern edge of the city, which was to be called *Ulrikasborg* (Ullanlinna). But as it was, both Helsinki and the kingdom of Sweden as a whole had suffered too much from the long period of wars to contemplate such a construction.

SVEABORG

During the real period of Swedish hegemony in the 17th century, the Baltic was virtually a national inland sea, as it was only the southern coast from Kurland and the areas belonging to Prussia, Poland and Germany to Denmark that was in alien hands. Russia had not had any direct outlet to the Baltic coast since 1617.

The accession of Emperor Peter I marked the beginning of a new era in Russian foreign policy and military affairs, a period which saw the extension of the country's territories to reach the shores of the Baltic Sea and the Black Sea and the creation of a navy on both of these. Peter's Baltic policy had a strong commercial and cultural aspect from the outset. A fortress built at St. Petersburg in 1703 and the bastion of Kronstadt on an island outside it protected the rapidly growing city, which superseded Moscow as the capital and administrative centre of the whole of Russia in 1712. The whole tone of the Gulf of Finland altered radically now that Russia had succeeded in reversing the direction of events following centuries of Swedish expansion eastwards. The Treaty of Uusikaupunki in 1721 then confirmed the Emperor's rights over Estonia, Livonia, Ingria (where he had founded the city of St.Petersburg), Karelia (including Vyborg) and the whole of the Lake Ladoga area – and granted him the title of *Imperator*. The borders defined in this treaty became the key to Russia's identity under her new security policy, and it was this border that Stalin set as his target in the wars between Finland and the Soviet Union in 1939–1945. In the end he was successful in this, as also in the case of the territories of Estonia and Livonia, which were lost by Russia again in 1991.

Thus a situation once more prevailed in which the two shores of the Gulf of Finland were in the hands of different powers, giving rise to a state of tension which led both to efforts at preserving peace and to the building of fortifications and the gathering of a navy on both sides. This was to have a considerable effect on the development of Helsinki.

In the general scheme of political alliances in Europe, the chief protagonist of Russia was Turkey, which had the support of France. Sweden, meanwhile, abandoned its policy of conciliation towards Russia in the 1730's and, under pressure from France, joined the French-Turkish front. This led it into a war of retribution against Russia in 1741, the aim of which was to recover the territories lost in the

Helsinki and its nearby islands formed an excellently protected harbour for use as a base once the border between Sweden and Russia had again been moved westwards to the Kymi River, in 1743, and Sweden, with the support of France and Turkey, was intent on mounting a new offensive to recover the lost territories, including Karelia and Estonia. Peter the Great had founded the city of St. Petersburg in 1703 and raised Russia to the status of a major maritime power in both the Baltic and the Black Sea.

Great Northern War. The war nevertheless ended in victory for Russia, and the boundary was moved further west, to the Kymi River. Sweden was intent on continuing with its existing alliances, however, and made preparations for new hostilities in the Gulf of Finland. The aim was to force Russia into a war on two fronts, against both Sweden and Turkey, and this is indeed what happened.

It is easy against this background to appreciate why it was in France's interests to pay large subsidies to Sweden, money which from 1748 onwards was spent mostly on constructing the fortress of *Sveaborg* (Suomenlinna) on the islands of *Vargskär* off the coast of Helsinki and fitting out a fleet to use it. The purpose of the operation was partly to prevent Russia from making any new attempts to occupy Finland, but above all to act as a base for mounting offensives against St. Petersburg.

Our correspondent Forsius wrote at the time of the building of Sveaborg:

Both experience and common sense would dictate that fortifications should be built in boundary regions, at least, so that the enemy can be prevented from entering the country and so that one's own forces can be gathered there to set out with brave hearts and plentiful supplies to attack the enemy.

Sveaborg, which was given the Finnish name *Suomenlinna* in 1918 and is now a UNESCO World Heritage monument, is a fascinating example of military architecture and the design of a large garrison headquarters. One essential feature of its original character that modern visitors do not experience, however, is the swarm of sea-going sailing ships of different sizes that must have surrounded it, particularly the typical light galleys that were well adapted to sailing among the coastal islands, the swirl of their sails, the noises and smells, and the bustle of the sailors.

Although Sveaborg was an expression of the European power politics of its day and a major object of military investment, it was in practice very much the achievement of one man. Augustin Ehrensvärd, a 37-year-old officer who had studied abroad and was well versed technically in matters of fortification and artillery, and in addition was of the correct political leanings, was entrusted with the task of directing the construction work. With short interruptions, this became his life's work for more than 20 years, at the end of which he was able to see the main part of the fortress completed. The overall plan for the fortification of the entire area was never put into effect. A decisive contribution was also made by the naval designer F. af Chap-

man, who directed the work of building a whole new fleet of light-weight vessels capable of operating among the islands.

Sveaborg was built, with subsidies from France, by troops recruited from all parts of the kingdom of Sweden, and this major investment inevitably added greatly to the economic importance of Helsinki and to its population. The social life of the officers at Sveaborg brought French culture to the islands of the Gulf of Finland and led to a certain Europeanization of the city and its hinterland.

Although the Russians devoted huge resources to the reinforcement of the fortress of Kronstadt and to fortifications and a naval presence in Tallinn, Sveaborg posed a permanent threat to them from the latter half of the 18th century onwards. In 1788 Sweden once more

Construction of the fortress of Sveaborg, by Finnish troops with financial assistance from France, began in 1748. The work went on for about thirty years and was never entirely finished, as no fortifications were ever built on the shore of Helsinki itself, and those on the islands east of Sveaborg remained incomplete.

19

The opposite number
to Sveaborg was the
fortress of Kronstadt
off St. Petersburg.
Work on this was
begun under Peter
the Great but it
was extended and
strengthened at
the same time as
Sveaborg was being
built, during the
reign of the Empress
Elizabeth.

attacked Russia, again in the hope of regaining its lost territories and, together with Turkey, of weakening Russia and causing internal divisions within it. This was above all a sea battle, the main engagements being around the island of Suursaari and off Kotka. Sweden was no more successful on this occasion, however.

When Napoleon's armies invaded Prussia in 1806–1807 and reached the shores of the Baltic Sea, Russia was forced to revise its policies, leading to the forming of an alliance sealed by the Treaty of Tilsit, on the border between Lithuania and Prussia, signed by Emperor Alexander I and the Emperor Napoleon in 1807. Under this agreement Russia was to join the trade war against England and the two powers were to strive for a division of the empire of the Turks. Russia was given a free hand to destroy Sweden, an ally of England, and Alexander I effectively gained victory over his "geographical enemy" in 1808 and announced that he was annexing Finland permanently to the Russian Empire. Here, again, the fortress of Sveaborg occupied a key position. It posed a threat which it was of the utmost importance to eliminate, and when it eventually capitulated in May 1808 after a protracted siege, a huge victory parade was staged in St. Petersburg and Russia expressed the hope that a salute would be fired in Paris as well in honour of the occasion.

The building of Sveaborg and the large numbers of troops stationed there ensured that Helsinki grew into a significant, if not yet very large, city by the latter half of the 18th century. Its culture was a natural continuation of that of Stockholm, an aristocratic society culture with its Freemasons' lodges, masquerades, novels and musical soirées. Its atmosphere was quite different from that of a bishop's see or a seat of learning such as Turku or Porvoo (Borgå). Many of the officers had served in the Royal Suédois regiment in Strasbourg, and conversations in Sveaborg centred around military affairs and world politics. Unlike the rural clergy and peasant farmers, who were royalists at heart, the officers supported the aspirations of the aristocratic opposition that gained expression in the motives of the Anjala League in 1789, during Gustavus III's war with Russia, and culminated in the king's assassination in 1792. Thus, thanks to Sveaborg, Helsinki was a political city even in the 18th century – the only one in the eastern part of the kingdom. On the other hand, it lost the status of administrative centre for the provinces of Uusimaa and Häme to Hämeenlinna in 1776, having been the seat of the governor from the time when the modern system of provinces in Sweden(-Finland) was created in 1635. It became a provincial capital again in 1831 (only to lose the status to Hämeenlinna once more in 1998).

Tersmeden, owner of the Alberga estate and an officer at Sveaborg, was apt to play cards both with his colleagues, including Ehrensvärd, and in the merchant circles of Helsinki, and his diary contains frequent observations of the kind: *The whole of the rest of the day was wasted on account of the visitor, at least as far as anything intelligent was concerned, as it went only on dancing and playing*, or simply *Pleasant company and cards*. The city also began to attract travelling theatrical companies, dancing instructors and language teachers.

Life of the officers at Sveaborg. The picture shows a military tribunal, with the scribes and the accused.

One of the young officers at Sveaborg was J.A. Ehrenström, who soon showed a preference for a political career. His father was a member of the minor aristocracy and a representative of the most modern branch of warfare, artillery, at Sveaborg, but his uncle was the richest man in Helsinki, the merchant Johan Sederholm, whose stone-built house still stands on the edge of the Great Square, or Senate Square. Ehrenström was to become one of the central figures in the process of transition, in Helsinki and in Finland in general, from the politics and intellectual culture of Gustavus III to the age of the Emperor Alexander I.

THE SENATE SQUARE'S TALE

Emperor Alexander I took over the major part of Finland in the early spring of 1808, and it was round about the same time that he gained control over Sveaborg. The war between Russia and Sweden was still going on in the north, however, and it was not until September 1809 that a peace treaty was eventually signed at Hamina. Under this agreement Sweden ceded all its provinces within Finland to Russia. Even before the treaty was signed, in fact, the Emperor had already formed these territories into a new Grand Duchy of Finland, the estates of which had assembled at Porvoo in the early spring of

Bust of Emperor Alexander I, "Father of the Homeland and its University", in the Great Hall of the university after its transfer to Helsinki. The work of the famous Russian sculptor I. Martos, the statue was removed from its position in the Great Hall at a time of nationalistic fervour in the 1930's.

that year. Even at that preliminary stage the question had been raised as to what city was to become the capital of this new constitutional entity.

The Emperor visited Sveaborg and Helsinki on 18th March 1809, as the sun shone brightly on the sea ice. His adjutant, the general Prince Gagarin, provides in his book an enthusiastic description of the might of this fortress, which "the lions of Sweden built for the eagles of Russia": the fortifications, which amounted to "a library of cannons", the impressiveness of the memorial to Ehrensvärd, and the harbour constructions, which were far stronger and more important than he had expected. The dinner and dance arranged by the merchants of Helsinki in the evening, on the other hand, he regarded as somewhat provincial.

The councillors and elders of this distinguished city did not scrimp on the number of courses served nor on the honours bestowed; but the fish became mixed up with the meat, and the meat with the seasoning. The olives and cucumber did not wait for the roast, but the currants came before the truffles and the truffles before the purée. The dessert was crowned with an orange, but shamefully aware of its deformity, as it had been caught by the frost, and this sweet, golden fruit had turned red and bitter. But among the other wines they served an old wine in old glasses, and what is more, it was a Rhine wine to which large cubes of sugar had been added. It was in this wine that we drank the toasts. – – The dancing in Helsinki was a hundred times better than the dinner – –.

Directly after the dancing the Emperor and his retinue left by night for Turku in horse-drawn sleighs. Gagarin's sleigh turned over at one point and he could sense that there were wolves not far away.

Finland had not constituted any kind of administrative or even psychological entity of its own during Swedish times, and if one had asked what its capital was, then the answer would naturally have been Stockholm. Each of the provinces on the Finnish side of the Gulf of Bothnia was in direct contact with Stockholm both administratively and fiscally, and innovations tended to spread by the same route. Now Finland suddenly found itself a separate geographical unit, at the same time as the Russian capital, St. Petersburg, emerged as a significant factor affecting its world, for this was where the ruler of Finland now resided, and it was necessary to set up a highly important Finnish constitutional body there, the office of the Secretary of State for Finland. Poland had the same kind of institution there at first, but for most of the Imperial period Finland was the only part of the Russian Empire that had its own Secretary of State's office in the imperial capital. At the same time a considerable migration of population from

Eastern Finland to St. Petersburg began, which had a permanent effect on Finnish urban traditions.

In 1812, when the decision was made to make Helsinki into the capital of Finland and to rebuild the city (following another fire) in a manner consistent with its new status, two other decisions of major importance were also taken. One of these involved the incorporation of Vyborg and its province, acquired by Russia at an earlier juncture, into the new Grand Duchy. This increased the spread of cultural and consumer habits from St. Petersburg and again promoted migration.

When Napoleon attacked Russia, Sweden did not join the attack, but preferred to sign the Turku Treaty of Friendship and Mutual Assistance, thereby finally abandoning its policy of retribution directed towards the east. This guaranteed a state of peace in the Baltic and the Gulf of Finland for a very long time to come, the situation altering only at the end of the century, when military, and particularly naval relations between Germany and Russia became more strained, eventually leading to the outbreak of the First World War. Russia had acquired control over Finland and Sveaborg with the security interests of St. Petersburg in mind, and with its coastal territories, its navy and its fortresses, there was no doubt that it enjoyed hegemony over the Baltic Sea virtually throughout the 19th century. This implied a military element in life at all times as far as Helsinki was concerned, but apart from the Crimean War in 1853–1856, actual hostilities were a distant prospect. Instead, the military garrison was above all an important economic factor for the city. In the early years after Helsinki had been declared the capital, a high proportion of the revenues of the Grand Duchy were devoted to its construction and the maintenance of its civil servants.

The combined British-French naval attack on Sveaborg in 1855 bore witness to the importance of Helsinki as the gateway to St. Petersburg. It also proved that the war was to be fought on all fronts and not only in Crimea, and that the ancient strategic connection between the Baltic and the Black Sea still existed. In this way Russia was forced to keep large numbers of troops in and around St. Petersburg.

The committee for the reconstruction of the city of Helsinki was headed by J.A. Ehrenström, former favourite of Gustavus III, who had travelled widely in Russia and Europe and was undertaking his new duties under the patronage of another former favourite of the King's, Count G.M. Armfelt, now a close advisor to Alexander I. The Emperor himself followed the progress of the project in terms of the planning and architecture, and his brother and successor (from 1825), Nikolai I, took a personal interest in the designing of the buildings. In 1816 the committee acquired the services of Carl Ludwig Engel, originally from Berlin, who had also acted as an architect in Tallinn and St. Petersburg. Not only was Engel given the unique task of designing an entire new administrative city – soon to become a university city as well, but he also became head of the national buildings committee, and as such was responsible for numerous town plans, churches and manor houses all over the country. In fact he gave the whole of Finland a new outward appearance.

Engel wrote at one point:

My most ardent wish appears to be coming true, as I have practically an unlimited field in which to exercise and use my talents, a situation which rarely befalls an architect, – – as it is a rare pleasure to be allowed to build a whole city.

Engel began by designing two large military barracks for the city – the present buildings of the General Headquarters of the Defence Forces and the Ministry of Foreign Affairs – and then a palace for the Governor General and a large building for the Imperial Senate, a small Orthodox church and a larger Lutheran church. He then began a long-term project for the building of a gigantic Church of St. Nicholas and also produced designs for hospitals and private houses. The great fire of Turku in 1827 provided a motive for transferring the old university to Helsinki, even though its buildings as such had not been destroyed in the fire. This meant that the already large and magnificent Senate Square could be filled in on the west side with a university building to match the monumental Senate building for size. This building was painted white in the Greek style while the Senate building was yellow in the Roman style. Other university buildings were also provided, notably an observatory, a glasshouse and facilities for various medical departments.

The fire and the loss of the university deprived Turku of the prestige that it had enjoyed up to that time (although Engel did design a fine new town plan for the city and some individual buildings as well, and although the seat of the Archbishop remained there and also one of the country's three courts of appeal). Meanwhile Helsinki developed from a garrison and administrative centre into a university centre and eventually a seat of learning on a broader scale. The transfer of the university to the administrative capital was consistent with the spirit of the times, as this was a period when the civil service increased greatly in numbers and its educational standards rose substantially. The central administration and the training of officials was all concentrated in Helsinki, from where they were able to exercise influence over the whole country. *You can't imagine how beautiful Helsinki will be, and how beautiful it is now*, Engel wrote in 1831, at a time when the university building was under construction and he was in the process of designing the university library – *the like of which no other university will be able to display*. Engel also developed into a specialist in stoves and heating systems during his career in Helsinki, and was even able to publish his designs in German architectural journals.

The professors of the University, the younger intellectuals and the students began from the 1830's onwards to develop a Finnish national ideology. By the time the University was ready to celebrate its bicentenary in 1840 the classical Senate Square was virtually complete and the recently founded semi-official Finnish Literature Society and Finnish Society of Science and Letters were already showing outward

The rebuilding of the city centre in an entirely new neo-classical style took place at the command of the Emperor himself and according to designs supplied by the Berlin-born architect C.L. Engel. The picture shows the main building of the Imperial Alexander University, the main guardhouse and the square which was cleared in the centre of what had been the old town. Opposite the university was a building of a similar size occupied by the Imperial Senate, and still used nowadays by the Council of State.

signs of intellectual activity. *Runeberg*, who created a classical ideal for the Finnish people and the natural environment of Finland, *Lönnrot*, who collected and compiled the national epic poem, the *Kalevala*, *Snellman*, whose influence on public debate and political thinking in Finland was so immense, *Cygnaeus*, who began the Finnish tradition in the arts and artistic education, and the somewhat younger *Topelius*, who became a favourite with the general public and young people through his historical novels and fairytales and emerged as a central figure in journalism and patriotic sentiment, all belonged to the University in the 1830's and remained active in its spheres in one way or another until the 1870's or later. At the same time, the university's German-born teacher of music, *Pacius*, was laying down high standards for Finland's musical traditions.

The University, the Senate, St. Nicholas' Church and the houses of the merchants and bankers on the south side of the Senate Square exercised a combined influence that permeated the whole country. Each in its own way epitomised the notion of *loyal autonomy* that was the key to the success of the Grand Duchy. The Senate Square as such, an open space cleared in the centre of the old 18th century town – with a great expenditure of labour in view of the difficulty of the earthworks involved – was a parade ground where divisions of the Imperial Army were able to march and proclaim the might of the Russian Empire.

Society life in Helsinki, maintained largely by the senators, the Russian military and the upper classes from St. Petersburg who spent the summer there, and also some circles in the University, flourished at that time; there were frequent visits by theatrical companies, dances were held and all manner of celebrations took place. A French traveller X. Marmier wrote in a book published in Paris in 1843:

The saloons of the aristocrats of Helsinki are just as elegant as their most beautiful counterparts in Paris, and the society circles that frequent them, Finnish in their hearts, Russian by force of circumstance and French in spirit and customs, display to the foreigner an unusual composition of ideas, with the old sympathies and traditions, their new aspirations and their many languages. In the course of one evening you can hear folk tales from the Tornio Valley, anecdotes from the Imperial court and the latest news from France. First they praise the singing of M. de Lamartine, then a naïve Finnish ballad, Swedish verses by Tegnér or the Russian elegies of Mdme. the Countess Rostopchin. An officer from a distant garrison tells of the wild tribes of Siberia or the Caucasus, one of the ladies tells of her recent journey to Italy, another passionately describes the banks of the Neva, and all the mélange of facts, analyses and cosmopolitan stories is quite enchanting.

One of the most successful of all Engel's architectural designs was the Library of the Imperial Alexander University, built in 1844. It consists of three main rooms, of which this Catalogue Room is the middle one.

Politics was the one thing that no one spoke about. Alongside this aristocratic life, these arose from the 1840's onwards an extensive political and national debate among the students and young intellectuals which reflected the social and ideological developments taking place on the continent of Europe. Admittedly the circles that fashioned opinions in Finland and those that gave expression to them frequently found themselves in situations in which they were expected to express interest and loyalty towards movements for freedom and revolution prevalent on the continent of Europe and at the same time loyalty to the Russian Empire, in the full knowledge that Finland's success and relatively privileged position in the Empire demanded utter reliability on the part of its citizens. After all, Russia had acquired Finland as a protection for its own capital city and could not permit any notions of revolution to circulate "at the gates of St. Petersburg". Finland could not be allowed to become a "new Poland", a seat of rebellion.

In fact, the Finns developed their own solution to this paradox, their own "national loyalty". As the price for external loyalty in matters of foreign policy, Finland gradually created a unique national identity of its own. Thus the response to the Polish rebellion of 1831 was the founding of the Finnish Literature Society, and the corresponding response to the revolutionary movement of 1848

The university and its students became the chief manifestation and core of the emerging modern Finnish nation. National opinion was gradually formulated in a constructive spirit and with distinct idealistic and aesthetic overtones. The university was also the cradle of Finnish music, under the guidance of the German-born Fredrick Pacius.

was the great students' spring festival at the Kumtähti stadium on the 13th May of that year, at which the future Finnish national anthem *Maamme* was sung and the Finnish flag flown for the first time. It was then that the Finland that had been born in 1809 achieved a national consciousness on modern lines.

The Crimean War brought the British and French squadrons to the Åland Islands to destroy the great castle of Bomarsund, to set fire to the coastal towns and merchant ships on the Gulf of Bothnia and to manifest their power in a mighty assault on Sveaborg that lasted uninterrupted for 46 hours. The ultimate target, of course, was St. Petersburg. Helsinki as such was not attacked, but the demonstration clearly had some influence, along with the defeat of Russia and the change of sovereign. Thus began the reign of a new, more liberal-minded Emperor, Alexander II (1855–1881), now commemorated by a statue in

Fredrick Pacius

Emperor Alexander II, in the company of his sons and the chief ministers of the Russian government, opened the Diet of 1863 in the Imperial Palace, although in an atmosphere sobered by the new revolt in Poland. Finland was the only part of the Russian Empire where parliamentary life functioned properly, although admittedly on the old-fashioned principle of representation of the four estates. This system was replaced by a Parliament with a single chamber in 1906, during the reign of Nikolai II.

the most prestigious place in the whole of Finland, the centre of the Senate Square.

In 1863 Finland again had to react appropriately to a major political crisis, a new rebellion in Poland. By this time liberal ideas had aroused much sympathy and an influential circle of people had established themselves who were prepared to emphasize Finland's special status vis-à-vis Russia and even to express hopes for a Finnish merchant marine flag. This moved the Emperor to summon a meeting of the Diet in Helsinki, although he also underlined the power of the Empire with a grand parade and his personal presence and thereby managed to achieve a consensus along moderate lines.

Helsinki now became not only the seat of the Senate and its bureaucracy but also the place of assembly for the Diet of the Estates, which met at regular intervals. The first building to be provided for this purpose was the large House of the Nobility, in a park behind the Senate building. It is perhaps symptomatic that this was no longer neo-Classic but built in red brick in the Gothic style.

After a long period of deliberation, an extremely elegant House of the Estates was later built north of the Senate and the Church of St. Nicholas for use by the three lower estates. Together with the buildings of the *Bank of Finland* and the National Archives, this forms another cluster of public buildings representing a different period from the imperial bureaucratism of the Senate Square.

The Bank of Finland assumed a significant status when Finland gained its own currency, the *markka* and *penni*, in 1860, and when this was freed from the rouble in 1865 and linked first to the silver standard and later, in 1878, to the gold standard.

A MULTICULTURAL CITY

During the Cold War period Helsinki served on many occasions as a Little St. Petersburg or a Substitute Moscow for American film teams. The architecture of the city, its visual character and physical environment and the naturally introverted behaviour of its people easily persuaded foreigners that it had more of the east about it than of the west. And geography easily led people to the same conclusion, as it is only 450 kilometres away from St. Petersburg and it is obvious that its government buildings and monuments will also give it the same atmosphere as its larger neighbour. The Uspensky Cathedral, which rises up on a level with the mightiest of all Helsinki landmarks, the Church of St. Nicholas, is in many people's eyes a magnificent sight, but definitely a symbol of eastern influence.

How did Helsinki gain its "Russian" air? The capital never underwent a process of Russification at any time, as its bureaucratic, academic and spiritual elite arose from among the Finns themselves. The main circumstances that led to the formation of this new class were undoubtedly the creation of a central administration and the

The Russian Theatre, or Alexander Theatre, on the Boulevard, was built in 1876, and it was here that the Finnish Opera, founded by Aino Ackté and Edward Fazer, gave its first performances in 1911. The area around the Boulevard constituted one of the first "suburbs" in Ehrenström's town plan.

transfer of the University to Helsinki. Both the civil and military administration provided work for the uppermost stratum in the system of estates, the aristocracy. It was this class that dominated the positions of power in the government and occupied the majority of the higher civil service posts. Thus the upper strata of society in general came to form the first urban elite of Helsinki, the officials, who in turn were arranged in a strict hierarchy. At the head was the Governor General, the Provincial Governor, the members of the Imperial Senate and the heads of departments in the central administration, while the civil service echelons attached to the Senate were headed by the permanent secretaries, followed by the protocol secretaries, the registrars and translators, the office secretaries, clerks and archivists, each in his own rank as graciously laid down in the Ordinance of 1826.

The surrender of Sveaborg in May 1808 meant the arrival of large numbers of Russian troops in Helsinki. The fortress became a Russian naval base under the command of Major General Constantin Gavro, which together with Kronstadt formed an important protective military zone outside St.Petersburg. And it was specifically a Russian base – it was not allowed to serve in any way as a base for the newly formed Finnish military forces. For this purpose the Guards Barracks beside the New City Square, the Naval Barracks on Katajanokka and the Turku Barracks beside the main road leading west to Turku were built. The officers lived in the town and made a visible and impressive contribution to the social life of the young capital. Reminders of the Russian period that are still to be seen on Sveaborg include the Church of St. Alexander Nevsky, built in the 1850's on medieval Byzantine lines as the main Orthodox church but rededicated as a Lutheran Church in the 1920's.

The events of the war in the east in 1854–55 had a profound effect on life in Helsinki. The fortifications on Sveaborg were strengthened and defence capabilities improved, and the numbers of Russian troops and naval units stationed there were increased. When the Anglo-French naval detachment opened fire on the fortress in August 1855, there were five grenadier battalions, Grodno hussars, fortress and field artillery units, and cavalry, cossack and sapper detachments billeted or encamped in Helsinki in addition to troops of the 22nd Infantry Division. The raids were disastrous for Sveaborg, however, and they meant the end of its history as a naval base. From that time onwards it served the needs of the land forces. A large barracks was built on the shore of the island of Iso Mustasaari around 1870, which became the Russian Gate to the fortress, and a host of Russian traders, tailors, cobblers and other artisans had their shops in the wooden houses behind it.

The next time that a powerful Russian military influence made itself felt in Helsinki was during the First World War, when about 25 000 men were stationed in the city. At the beginning most of these troops were men of the 427th and 428th Infantry Regiments, fortress and field artillery and Don Cossacks. The Baltic Fleet of the Russian Navy was represented by a liner brigade, a fleet of torpedo boats, part of a cruiser brigade and a minesweeper detachment. The Russian troops were both visible and influential in Helsinki in the turbulent times towards the end of the First World War.

The merchants of 19th-century Helsinki formed numerous groups in terms of language, wealth, lines of business and nationality. The uppermost level in the hierarchy consisted of those engaged in domestic and foreign trade, who were in the minority even though they formed a majority in the city's administration. The Russian-born element stood out from this group by virtue of their high tax contributions, their influence being at its peak around the middle of the century. Many familiar names can be traced back to that period: Sinebrychoff, Kiseleff, Kudrakoff, Uschanoff and Koroleff, for instance. The permanence of this elite was strengthened further by the general lack of social mobility and the lack of social contacts between the various merchant groups. Among the industrial families, the Sinebrychoffs, who founded the brewery, and the Kiseleffs, who were instrumental in starting a sugar refinery and a gasworks, gradually became absorbed into Helsinki society in the course of the century.

The largest and most conspicuous group of Russians was the small traders, houseowners, gardeners and above all provision merchants, whose colourful little shops, delicatessens and "lavka" were an essential feature of the Helsinki street scene. Here you could buy just about anything, from grain and sponges to bamboo fishing rods. The first pioneers of market gardening in Helsinki were Russians, as were many of the small traders selling goods in the streets and markets. The street trade in ice-cream at the end of the last century was almost entirely in the hands of Russian manufacturers, and cries of "Kharoshi maroshi" were an essential feature of summer in the capital.

The most obvious external marks of the Orthodox Church, which founded a parish of its own in Helsinki in 1827, were the Church of the Holy Trinity (1827), the Uspensky Cathedral (1868) and the Chapel of Peace, consecrated in 1913 to mark the centenary of the Treaty of Hamina but later demolished. For a long time the parishioners were Russian-born military and civil service staff or merchants. Their cul-

The Uspensky Cathedral, "the city's most striking Orthodox church", was consecrated in 1868. The part of the city surrounding it, known as Katajanokka, was built mostly within a short space of time at the beginning of the 20th century, in the prevailing national romantic style.

tural life tended to centre around the Alexander Theatre in the Boulevard, which enjoyed its first golden age around the turn of the century, when numerous well-known theatrical groups from St. Petersburg performed there. It was in this same theatre that the Finnish opera company founded by Aino Ackté and Edward Fazer held its first performance in 1911, and the same building continued to be the home of the Finnish Opera until the 1990's. It is now maintained by Helsinki City Council as a venue for visiting performers.

The city was in all respects a multilingual and multicultural place in Imperial times, and housed a multifarious population. The Russian military brought with them many kinds of "non-Finnish subordinates" – as the statistical category used in 1875 puts it – who differed from the main population of the city in nationality and religion at least. The history of the Roman Catholic Church in Helsinki goes back to the Crimean War, when a group of soldiers, mainly of Polish origin, decided to form a parish of their own and gained support in this from the Governor General, Count Berg, whose Italian-born wife was a Roman Catholic. The church, dedicated to Finland's own martyr from the Catholic era, St. Henrik, was built in the Kaivopuisto area in 1860.

The first Jews came to Helsinki on the heels of the Russian military, as the regulation going back to Swedish times that forbade Jews to live in Finland did not apply to people in the service of the Russian army. Since this service could last as long as 25 years, a soldier and his family could easily develop roots in the place where he was stationed. Thus a decree was issued in 1858 that granted soldiers of the Russian army in general, provided they were in possession of demobilization papers, a passport or some other valid travel document, the right to reside in Finland and to make a living here by selling handicrafts that they had made, bread, berries, cigarettes or second-hand clothes and other goods. Eventually a separate Jewish market known as Narinkka (Russ. *na rynke* = at the market) grew up, which at a later stage functioned in the Simonaukio square, close to the present Bus Station. A number of well-known Jewish families can be traced back to the early years of the 1870's, notably the Drisin, Rung, Skurnik and Stiller families. Helsinki became the centre for the Jewish community in Finland

Aurora Karamzin (1808-1902), who was invited to St. Petersburg to serve as a lady-in-waiting at the Imperial court, was one of the best-known Finnish society beauties in her day. She was married twice and devoted much of her wealth to charity. She gave generous support to the elementary school system, nursing, child welfare and care of the poor, and founded the Deaconess' Institute in 1867. Her Helsinki home, the Hakasalmi Villa, has been in the possession of the City Museum since 1912.

from the outset, and the country's entire Jewish population amounted to about a thousand by 1890. A synagogue in Malminkatu, designed by the architect J. Ahrenberg, was consecrated in 1906, and meeting rooms, a kindergarten and school rooms etc. were added in 1962.

The first Muslims to come to Helsinki also did so in connection with the Russian garrison and the fortification and improvement work carried out at Sveaborg. The earliest mention of them is from 1853. With the granting of freedom of occupation, other enterprising artisans from Finland and abroad were attracted to Helsinki by the commercial and industrial opportunities it offered. Towards the end

A Mohammedan religious service in Helsinki in the late 19th century.

of the Imperial period the first Tatars also came. These, too, were merchants, and many of the city's furriers and older clothing shops are still owned by their descendants. Once the Law on Religious Freedom was passed in 1920 it became possible for them to form their own religious community, which was registered in 1925. As it gained in affluence, the congregation functioning in Helsinki acquired two properties in Fredrikinkatu, and Islam House was finally built on the corner of Fredrikinkatu and Uudenmaankatu in 1960. An Islamic cemetery was opened in the Lapinlahti district in the late 19th century.

The Germans, who formed an independent group within the merchant community, founded a separate Lutheran Parish of their own in the 1850's. Although their numbers have never been particularly large, German-born families have had a considerable influence on the city's economic and cultural life. Many notable factories, shops, restaurants and hotels were originally founded by Helsinki Germans, the names of whom still survive 150 years later. Stockmann, Fazer, König, Kämp, Kleineh, Osberg, Staudinger, Wulff, Paulig, Knief, Schröder, Bargum and many more have left a permanent mark on life in the city, as also have the music professor Pacius, the philanthropist Sedmigradsky and the architect Lohrmann. The German church in Unioninkatu provides firm evidence of the living influence of this community.

The cosmopolitan life of the Imperial period was also marked by the first instances of tourism in Helsinki. Travel between the Finnish capital and St. Petersburg became very much quicker once regular steamship services were inaugurated in 1837, and again when the railway was completed in 1870. The earliest golden age of tourism was thus in the 1840's, when the general political situation in Europe favoured travel by Russians within their own country. The small, elegant city of Helsinki had a rustic air about it. It was peaceful and close to nature, and this helped it to become a popular place for spending the summer. The steamships played an important part in this tourist traffic, especially as far as visitors to the new spa opened in Kaivopuisto in May 1838 were concerned. The regular boat service and the beautiful spa setting created, as if by magic, out of the bare sea shore gave rise to a veritable flood of tourists, and the 1840's saw a boom in advertising on behalf of Helsinki and Finland in general and in the publishing of guidebooks for visitors.

The earliest tourist attraction in the city was thus created on the southern promontory of Vironniemi, with its rocky outcrops and intervening boggy patches. The first stage was to transform the rocky terrain into smooth, green parkland, a formidable process that was initiated by the privately owned spa company founded in 1834 and took

The park of Kaivopuisto and its spa made Helsinki into a favourite tourist attraction in the 1830's and 1840's. Wealthy families from St. Petersburg would come here in the summer, taking advantage of the regular steamship services. The park soon gained numerous villas offering accommodation for the summer visitors. Although the heyday of the spa as such remained relatively short-lived, Kaivopuisto is still a popular place for holding outdoor events in spring and summer.

nine years to complete. Innumerable loads of rock, landfill material, soil and sand were brought to the site, land drains were dug, pools built and trees and other vegetation planted. As early as 1839, Jakob Grot, later to become professor of Russian literature at the University, was moved to remark, "As far as its enchanting position is concerned, it promises to be a wonderful place for walks."

The actual spa building was erected on the southern shore of the Ullanlinna area in 1835, to a design by Engel, and the following year the company decided to build a pump house next door to it for those who wished to take the mineral waters as a health cure. Responsibility for distribution of the water was entrusted to P. A. von Bonsdorff, professor of chemistry and Victor Hartwall, who between them had founded a factory in Helsinki in 1836 for the manufacture of artificial mineral waters. As the business expanded it came into the hands of Hartwall alone, who was granted a licence by the Senate, also in 1836, "for the manufacture and sale to the public of all manner of artificial mineral waters, whether warm or cold" under the supervision of the National Board of Medicine. This was the beginning of the present-day Hartwall beverages company. The original restaurant is still in existence, but the spa was destroyed by the bombing of 1944.

The spa and pump house were opened to the public in June 1836,

and it meant that Helsinki had acquired its own place of recreation on the southern model, named Kaivopuisto, the Well Park. As a consequence, a motley assortment of visitors began to appear in the city: "There were millionaires who playfully handed out money to the astonished bystanders, and dandies who spent unbelievable sums on dances, fireworks and luxurious living", but there were also those who came out of thrift, since consumer goods were for a long while cheaper in Helsinki than in St. Petersburg. The Russians were attracted by the dreamy calm of the city, its unspoiled nature and its rustic urbanity. The Russian author Thaddeus Bulgarin wrote in 1838: "I am convinced that when the wealthier people (those of St. Petersburg) have been here once they will want to move from their cold, damp summer residences to the healthy surroundings of Finland, which are in their own way so attractive in their natural beauty."

As the visitors wished to live as near to the spa as possible, the spa company began in the early 1830's to distribute plots of land in the park area to those who wanted them, with the proviso that they should build villas on them. In no time at all eight such villas had grown up on the road leading to Kaivopuisto, and more were under construction nearby. The unrivalled star of the society life of the spa, the immensely rich Princess Yusupoff, had her villa built on the promontory of Rauhanniemi, "In a peculiar style of its own, the advantages of which we have not yet been able to fathom out", as Topelius put it. The house known as Kalliolinna, "The Castle on the Rock", built in 1844 for Johan Rabbe, manager of the spa, is also a spectacular reminder of the splendour conferred on Helsinki by this early period of tourism. Although the golden age came to an end in the 1850's, Kaivopuisto has retained its position as the principal venue for summer events in the city, most of all for open air concerts. Similarly the people of the city gather there regularly on 1st May to celebrate the arrival of spring.

THE THEATRE, STUDENT HOUSE
AND STOCKMANN

The Diet gave rise to certain parallel phenomena, in a way, in the form of the *New Theatre*, now known as the Swedish Theatre, built 1860–65, and the *Student House*, completed in 1870. The theatre was an essential even in Helsinki, as a world for the public life of the merchant classes, a place where the philosophy of the times and the bourgeois life of entertainments were able to come into their own both on the stage and in the foyer. For a long time the theatre in Helsinki was reliant entirely on visiting companies, mostly from Stockholm, but also from St.Petersburg, especially ballet groups in the summer time. As the public was limited, most plays were performed only a few times, the repertoire was changing constantly and artistic standards were naturally not especially high. This did mean, however, that European novelties,

Eduard Berents tyska trupp spelar sommaren 1873 "Sköna Helena" på Arkadiateatern. – Affisch HUB.

The Arcadia Theatre, which is usually remembered as the main forum for the performing of Finnish plays, also produced lighter works, which were much needed at the time. The programme for the 1873 production of Offenbach's La Belle Hélène is in Swedish, German and Russian.

particularly French comedies, came to the attention of the public in Helsinki relatively quickly. The operettas of Offenbach, for instance, were usually seen here within a year or so of their first night.

There was also some criticism of the accent placed on entertainment value in the theatrical world, and efforts were made to gather together a repertoire of Finnish works and to demand more serious drama. The rising ideology of *Fennomania* in particular came out against the "indecency" of the theatre – even to the extent of student demonstrations, and Finnish-language productions tended from the very beginning, in the 1870's, to adopt a much more serious-minded tone and a role as a morally edifying branch of art, although the next decade was already one of greater realism and the conveying of a clearer social message.

Operetta gained ground in the early years of the 20th century, especially in the summer theatres, but by that time Helsinki had so many theatres, restaurants and other places of entertainment that much was being written and said in novels and in public debate about the wanton consumption of the bourgeois and their loose habits. The city had become a place of confrontation between the urban liberal-bourgeois philosophy of life, Fennomania, with its roots in rural values and its emphasis on social issues, and socialism, which was gradually adopting the doctrine of the class struggle. The resulting ideological debate was carried on mostly within the University and in student circles.

When the University moved from Turku to Helsinki in 1828, its traditional provincial student fraternities, or *nationes*, rapidly took on a new meaning. At first they became focal points for the development and manifestation of a romantic patriotism, a Finnicism derived from the *Kalevala* and Runeberg. The young people spent their time engrossed in their written albums, singing flourished among the students and monarchism and patriotism were the order of the day. By the 1840's the more radical philosophies being propounded in Europe came to be reflected in the rapid adoption of contemporary political themes, the reading of newspapers and the founding of them on an amateur basis, and revision of the existing modes of assembly. Emphasis was still placed on traditional patriotism in the revolutionary year of 1848, mostly as a kind of defensive gesture, and as a consequence both the University and Finland in general managed to avoid any repressive measures on the part of the government. The *nationes* were suspended – for the time being – on account of their "anarchistic", i.e. political, character, and the government announced its intentions to encourage more career-oriented attitudes on the part of the

Helsingfors · Helsinki ,, Studenthuset · Ylioppilastalo.

Hälsning från "Studis."

11/11/1902.

gstedt & Näther, ljustryckeri, Hamburg. 12.

The Student Union building on the corner of Aleksanterinkatu and the present-day Mannerheimintie is perhaps the most important single building in the history of the Finnish nation as such. Funds were collected for it throughout the country from the beginning of the reign of Alexander II onwards, and the building was completed in 1870, the same year when the railway line to St. Petersburg was opened.

students. At the same time the degree courses were to be modernized, studies in the natural sciences were encouraged, and chairs were created in the Finnish language and Finnish history.

The need to accommodate the libraries of the former *nationes*, the new student faculties, the student music associations, the student newspaper club and the student restaurant led to the leasing of a building for this purpose, and in 1858 a campaign was launched to collect funds for the building of their own Student House. The project bore fruit in 1870, when the building now known as the *Old Student House* was opened with impressive ceremonies. Support had been received from all over the country, and in recognition of this the upper frieze on the façade was adorned with the famous inscription *Spei Suae Patria Dedit*, "a gift from the Motherland to its future hope". The Student House was the first significant building in Helsinki to embody the spirit of a national society and the mobilizing of the people in the form of a specific organization. It was destined to provide a venue for all manner of ideological and political activity, musical performances, theatre and all the other manifestations of the very diverse student life of the capital.

The students themselves had already enjoyed for a long time an established role of giving expression to public opinion and interpreting the *national mood*. They had become an element in the political life of the country, and as the Diet met infrequently, the debate carried on in student circles and the spectrum of parties that evolved from it occupied an important position. It was in the context of the student world that the whole of the future civil service and other leadership learned to form opinions of their own, to align themselves with political parties, to act in a corporate manner in societies and associations, to make speeches and to love their country – and alongside this to make friends and have a good time.

The Student House was located on the edge of the city at the time when it was built, but the centre soon shifted in that direction, so that the students were in possession of a very valuable site. In 1910 the Student Union invested in a new building next door to this, intended for use by the *nationes* and as a source of business income. Known as the New Student House, this is still mainly used for student organizations and social activities in the very centre of the city. Around the same time, too, the provincial student fraternities of Uusimaa and Ostrobothnia erected buildings of their own, both of which became major centres for social life and entertainments, but at the same time also arenas for ideological and political activity. Student life was primarily a matter of academic work, of course, but always with an important ingredient of mutual learning in matters of social significance.

The building of the Student House coincided almost exactly with the dawn of the new parliamentary age and the construction of the railway. All these things formed part of the transformation of Helsinki from a garrison town and seat of administration and learning to a complex modern city with accents on democracy, the press, business activity, urban middle-class values and the emergence of an industrial working population.

Another sign of a shift in the location of the city centre was the moving of the Stockmann department store from beside the Senate Square, next to the University, to a position close to the Student House and the Swedish Theatre. The two largest bookshops in the city, Akateeminen Kirjakauppa and Suomalainen Kirjakauppa, also moved to the same area, and the offices of the main newspapers, *Helsingin Sanomat, Uusi Suometar* – *Uusi Suomi* and *Hufvudstadsbladet*, were already located close by, as were the major publishing houses WSOY and Otava and their smaller Swedish-language equivalents Söderström & Co. and Holger Schildts Förlag.

The new Stockmann premises became the symbol of modernity in their day, with lifts and escalators, and with an entirely new approach to advertising, window-dressing and customer service. The building and everything that went on in it reflected well the views of the significant Helsinki architect and modernist theoretician S. Frosterus. The Stockmann family being of German origin – very many of the principal Helsinki shopkeeping families were of either German or Russian descent – the new building was closely related in spirit to the brick architecture of Hamburg and Berlin.

Visits to Stockmann's became an important part of the Helsinki way of life, and this came to be reflected in later department stores. The abundance of modern goods was another symbol of a new age, and now one was always likely to meet up with friends or catch a glimpse of celebrities, as had been the case with the market place in earlier times. As the suburbs began to grow in size, Stockmann's was a place that all suburban children learned to recognise and from where they could begin their mental conquest of the city centre.

Stockmann's also became famous in the 1930's as the place where diplomats accredited to Moscow and other foreigners living there would come to do their shopping. And if there was no time to travel, they could always order "western" goods from cloth to foodstuffs and from refrigerators to motor cars which were not to be had in the Soviet Union. When Russia was going through its great period of change in the early 1990's and Russian visitors began to flock through the streets of Helsinki once again, the large stores in the centre, with Stockmann at their head, went back to serving customers in Russian as well, just as in Tsarist times.

The mighty Stockmann department store, designed in the German style by Sigurd Frosterus and built at roughly the same time as the huge, classical Parliament House, overshadowed the Student House and other surrounding buildings and caused the focus of the central business district in Helsinki to shift from the eastern end of Aleksanterinkatu to the western end.

TWO FACES OF HELSINKI:
SÖRNÄINEN AND THE ESPLANADES

"*To the south lies the Helsinki of Ehrenström and Engel, which stands for the traditional order, senators, professors, the Book of our Land, doric columns, theatres, the opera, goldsmiths and places of education. To the north are the factories, the working people, cleaning rags, machine oil, steam, wood-fired stoves and windows spattered with blood.*"

(*Matti Kurjensaari:* The Tale of Helsinki, 1962)

Even today the Esplanades of southern Helsinki and Sörnäinen on the other side of Pitkäsilta, the long bridge, form two distinct parts of the city, two quite different urban ways of life and mentalities. Both have their roots in the first period of vigorous growth that Helsinki went through in the 1870's and 1880's, when people started moving from the countryside into the city in the hope of a better future. The city's population of 32 000 in 1870 was almost trebled over the next 30 years, and the same trend continued unabated for the first three decades of the 20th century. Thus there were about 250 000 people living there by the beginning of the Second World War. The progressive industrialization and the increase in the working-class population also meant that the capital became more Finnish in character, whereas about 40% of the population at the end of the 19th century had been Swedish-speaking.

The Helsinki that had been proclaimed capital of the Grand Duchy of Finland at the beginning of the century was a city of civil servants, military officers, men of learning and artisans, and there were scarcely any factories or large industrial concerns, but the enormous growth in population in the 1870's demonstrated that the size of the community and the diversity of the trades carried on in it had raised it to a new category, that of a major city. The number of industrial enterprises and the number of people employed in them had doubled, the large banks and insurance companies had become firmly established and instruction had begun to be given in technology. Department stores and hotels had been opened and restaurants and coffee shops had started up.

The built-up area expanded enormously, and both residential and industrial buildings spilled over into the areas of fields and pastures, villas and estates on the outskirts of the city, so that rock and stone was blasted by the tonne to make way for streets and buildings. A new working class community began to develop in the area north of Pitkäsilta from 1870 onwards, a community which by the turn of the century had a population equivalent to that of the whole of Helsinki 50 years earlier. There were two main factors that led to this growth: the extension of the Helsinki-Hämeenlinna railway to the promontory of Sörnäinen and the rebuilding of the main thoroughfare to the east, now known as Hämeentie, as this road linked the vast economic community of the capital with the eastern and northern parts of Uusimaa and the prosperous Häme region.

The railway, the highway, the trams, a china factory, large machine workshops producing goods for export, a tannery and an up-to-date wallpaper factory were all manifestations of the commencement of a new era and a new way of life. The Sörnäinen area began its age of glory, an age that was also marked by the discovery of the Finnish forests, as the 1870's was without doubt the decade of the Finnish timber trade. The first railway line in Finland to serve a harbour was built to the tip of the peninsula of Sörnäinen, where a new wharf was constructed, together with a variety of railway station and warehouse buildings. Soon private companies and traders were renting land and building warehouses of their own in the area. Sörnäinen became a

The growth of the city gathered momentum from the 1870's onwards, with the opening of the harbour at Sörnäinen and the building of new working-class housing in the Kallio district. The "line" layout of the streets and the monumental church, designed by Lars Sonck, are the landmarks of this part of the city.

Trading has been going on in the Market Place since the 18th century. The Esplanade, Market Place and South Shore form the maritime area of Helsinki. The building that is now the City Hall once housed the Seurahuone Hotel. Other buildings looking out over the Market Place include the Swedish Embassy, the Supreme Court and the Presidential Palace.

wild, motley place, the Klondyke of Helsinki, growing quickly and unconventionally. The railways were being extended to meet up with the great inland waterways. Timber was exported and oil was imported. Whole logs were transported direct from Lake Päijänne to Sörnäinen for shipping to the outside world.

The area north of Pitkäsilta developed into the largest industrial centre in the country, where the working-class population could create a political and cultural world of their own. The building and renting out of housing became a profitable occupation in the Kallio area of the city, where most of the rented accommodation was in wooden tenements which retained something of the spirit of living in the

countryside. The streets containing these buildings were known as 'lines', and the original intention was to build nine of these in parallel. The majority of the people living north of Pitkäsilta at the beginning of the 20th century were wage-earners, factory workers, unskilled labourers, manual workers and skilled building workers. It was only in 1901 that the area was actually incorporated into Helsinki itself, as ward no. IX, and the construction of larger brick buildings began in earnest.

By contrast, the southern part of Helsinki was growing all the time into a bourgeois urban area centred around the present-day Esplanade Park. Every large European city has its own fashionable street which

51

throbs with metropolitan life: the Champs-Elysées in Paris, Unten den Linden in Berlin and Kungsträdgården in Stockholm. And Helsinki has its Esplanades, which have retained an affectionate place in the hearts of the Helsinki people through the years. Their hotels, restaurants, coffee bars and shops are an inseparable part of people's collective memories of the heart of the capital. This is still the place to be seen in and to show yourself off in, the best urban stage in the city. The Esplanades have been praised and photographed and painted; they have been written about and sung about.

The present-day North Esplanade reflects in a nutshell the growth of Helsinki from a small Russian provincial town to a commercial centre. In its original form it marked the border between the stone-built and wooden parts of the town, and the open space for the park between the streets was designed as a border zone separating two rows of wooden buildings. The whole complex was intended as a residential area for the merchants and officials, who were allowed to build stone or brick houses along the North Esplanade but only wooden ones beside the southern one, as this was for a long time deemed to constitute a suburb of the city proper. The Esplanade, the Market Place and the South Shore formed an impressive, unified urban architectural whole, as Ehrenström had intended in his town plan of 1814.

The buying and selling of foodstuffs had been transferred from the Senate Square to the Market Place in 1818, and it was from there that most of the people of the city bought most of their food right up until well after the Second World War. Like the other markets in the capital, the Market Place itself was still entirely the province of the country folk and the fishermen at the end of the 19th century. The fishermen sold their wares straight from their boats, and the country farmers from open boxes and baskets set out on their market stalls. There was everything imaginable for sale: milk, freshly baked bread, fresh meat, salted, smoked and fresh fish, vegetables, live chickens and cockerels, fruit and berries. Handicrafts and hand-made wooden articles of all kinds were also sold. The Herring Market, a tradition that goes back to the 18th century, is still a regular event every autumn, with its own seafaring atmosphere.

The Market Place has always been an important venue for the people of Helsinki to meet and buy and sell their goods, and the bustle of the market somehow belongs to the seaside surroundings. Although retail trading has become far more developed and diversified nowadays, the Market Place has retained its position in the eyes of both the local people and the tourists. It has just as colourful an atmosphere, even though the selection of goods may no longer be what it was in the 1880's, when one observer described a Sunday market in the following words: "They had everything on sale that a working man could possibly want: brown Russian boots, trousers, jackets, shirts etc. You could buy, sell or exchange razors and have your beard trimmed or your hair cut. There was all sorts of under-the-counter stuff and home-made stuff, but no vodka, as that was looked down on, as it were. The men would scarcely sell any at all, but some old women might have a bottle or two and you could get some from them if you happened to run out and couldn't get to the government's shop in time."

Attention began to be drawn to the poor standards of hygiene in the market during the 1860's, and demands were voiced for "covered bazaars" instead of the open market stalls. Eventually the first market hall in Finland was designed by the architect Gustaf Nyström and erected in 1889 on the site in the Market Place where ready-cooked food had traditionally been sold. Ever since the 1830's there had been a small kitchen building there with stalls around it from which you could buy meat soup, pea soup, herring salad, gruel, porridge and warm water flavoured with syrup.

The first block of the North Esplanade to be built was the one that extends from the Market Place to Fabianinkatu, which possesses the clearest indicators of the old Tsarist style. For a long time the North

The old Market Hall was the first one of its kind in Finland.

53

Esplanade was lined with low stone or wooden buildings of two or three storeys. The centre part of the Esplanade, between Fabianinkatu and Mikonkatu, gained the air of an authentic European city during the years of rapid urban growth in the 1880's and 1890's, when the land was reinforced and splendid, elegant bourgeois stone buildings were put up, including the Catan Building (1890), the Hotel Kämp (1887) and the Grönqvist Building (1882), all designed by the architect Theodor Höijer. The last of these was the largest dwelling house and commercial building in the Nordic Countries at the time of its completion, and it was used at one stage for the first offices of the Helsinki Telephone Company.

The central part of the Esplanade, which was complemented in 1890 with the Mercurius Building designed for commercial use by Selim A. Lindqvist, thus became the heart of Helsinki and the centre of

The Esplanade Park is the most continental of Helsinki's public places. Many magnificent town houses were built along the Northern and Southern Esplanades from the 1880's onwards, and it was beside this park that the city's oldest theatre, the Hotel Kämp and the Kappeli Restaurant were located. Helsinki's first public monument, a statue of the poet Runeberg, was unveiled here in 1885.

its social life. The first public statue in the city, unveiled in May 1885, was similarly located in the Esplanade Park. This commemorated the national poet Runeberg. By the end of the century the Esplanade as a whole was becoming increasingly clearly divided into three parts, the Chapel section, the Runeberg section and the Theatre section. The first actual theatre building had been completed at the western end of the Esplanade in 1827. This was a yellow-painted wooden building situated in the shade of a semi-circle of maple trees. This fairly modest building which nevertheless provided so many excitements for the people of its time had been designed by the court architect C.L. Engel.

The theatre featured large numbers of first performances of Finnish plays, and the première of the first Finnish opera, *King Charles' Hunt*, in 1852, was celebrated by the whole city in the presence of the com-

poser and librettist, Fredrik Pacius and Zacharias Topelius. The present theatre and restaurant building was built in 1866, to plans drawn up by Nikolai Benois, a member of the Russian Academy of Art. The building has been refurbished on numerous occasions, but the Swedish Theatre, which occupies it nowadays, very aptly continues the long tradition of theatrical performances in Swedish on that site. The old wooden theatre building was moved away to a site on the edge of the city as it was at that time, in the present-day Arkadiankatu, where it became the Arkadia Theatre, the first permanent Finnish-language theatre.

Three restaurants have left their mark on the Esplanades in their time and have provided a basis for entertainments in the city. The pace was set by the Hotel Seurahuone, on the North Esplanade close to the Market Place. This was the oldest of the three, and opened its doors in 1833. The building for this centre of society life and entertainment was designed by C.L. Engel, and for a long time it was the largest and most magnificent hotel and restaurant complex in the country. The grandeur of its lines was apparent in the interior, too, for it had an amazingly big, opulent dining room and the hotel rooms were notably spacious. Apart from travellers, the Seurahuone extended its pleasures and comforts to civil servants, army officers, professors and even students. It became famous above all for its huge social gatherings, dances, masquerades, music and varieties. It was also a meeting place for discussion groups and gaming parties. The unforgettable crowning glory in its career was the bicentenary celebration of the Imperial Alexander University. The dance and other festivities went on for five days altogether and were attended by 1400 guests.

The Seurahuone did a lot to enliven the cultural life of the city as well. The main dining room was large enough for music and singing, and many significant works in the history of Finnish music had their first performance there. At best the room could accommodate an audience of about two thousand. It was there, too, that the popular concerts arranged by the Helsinki Orchestral Society (later the Helsinki City Orchestra) first began in 1882, under the direction of Robert Kajanus. The lease on the Seurahuone premises ran out in 1913, however, and was not renewed, as the City Council needed the space for its own purposes. The same block then became the focal point for the city's administration, and has been renovated and altered radically several times in recent decades.

In spite of the closure of the Seurahuone, the restaurant tradition in the Esplanade lives on in the form of the Kappeli (Chapel) Res-

taurant, one of the oldest Helsinki restaurants still functioning on its original site. The first building to be erected there was a kiosk built in the shape of a temple that sold soft drinks, cakes and pastries. This was opened in 1840. The Market Square end of the Esplanade Park was in fact a fenced enclosure with park benches and was intended as a place where the gentlefolk could take a walk. After about ten years it was realised that there was a great need for a restaurant there. The old kiosk had been so well used that contemporaries claimed it looked more like a dilapidated chicken run than a temple.

In practice it was another 17 years before the people were able to celebrate the opening of a new restaurant there in 1867. The big, light dining room of the Kappeli and the smaller pavilions leading off it provided a comfortable haven in the centre of the city. The restaurant became so popular, in fact, that additions were made to it before the end of the century. The first bandstand in the city was built opposite it in 1887, and it was this that gave rise to the tradition of open-air concerts in the Esplanade. Kappeli became the number one place to go in Helsinki in the summer and a favourite with the artistic community. It was ornately decorated, and many celebrated artists had contributed to its interior. The front gable is still embellished with a fanci-

The spacious, elegant dining room of the Seurahuone Hotel beside the Market Place was the scene of many Helsinki celebrations in the 19th century, and the beginnings of musical life in the city lay in the concerts held in this room.

ful female figure, the restaurant's own symbol, carved by the sculptor Walter Runeberg.

The youngest of the traditional restaurants in the Esplanade was the five-storey luxury hotel Kämp, built by the wealthy and energetic industrialist F.W. Grönqvist. Kämp was the surname of the first manager of the hotel. The restaurateur Carl Kämp had realized in the 1880's that Helsinki needed a high-class hotel and spacious restaurant that was well equipped for larger festivities and all kinds of meetings and celebrations, particularly in view of the expansion in industry and commerce. The railway network, which now extended to St. Petersburg, Kuopio and almost to Oulu, and the various steamship services, were bringing visitors to the city, and the businessmen and financiers of the Esplanades and Aleksanterinkatu needed a place to meet. At its opening in 1887, four hundred invited guests admired the expensive interiors, in which the influence of St. Petersburg styles was clearly visible. They were enraptured by the furniture upholstered in gilded leather, the elegant painted ceilings and the hydraulic lift. Crystal chandeliers that worked partly by electricity and partly by gas had been imported from Berlin. The hotel had 75 bedrooms, some with windows opening onto the inner courtyard and some onto Kluuvikatu or the Esplanade. It was at the Kämp that the decision was made to found the first Finnish-speaking bank, Kansallis-Osake-Pankki, in 1889. By the turn of the century the Kämp was far more than a hotel; it was the centre of the throbbing social life of a youthful capital. The people of Helsinki felt at home in the ground floor restaurant, and in the evening they would move to the Mirror Room upstairs. For a short time the building also housed one of the first cinemas in the city, the Helikon, opened in 1910. It also had a lively programme of varieties, operettas, comic songs and duets, musical comedies and conjurors, and frequent cabarets and Bellman evenings. It was for a long time the most European of the city's restaurants, with many of its managers, chefs and head waiters coming from St. Petersburg, Stockholm or the major cities on the continent. Its last evening, in 1965, came to an end with the pianist playing a melody by its most famous client, Sibelius, entitled "I'm going back to the Kämp". The building was demolished and replaced with a partial replica, which became the head offices of Kansallis-Osake-Pankki. The fully renovated Kämp returned to its original function as a hotel and restaurant in spring 1999, after an interval of over 30 years.

The mascot of Helsinki, a fountain and mermaid statue known as Havis Amanda, commissioned by the City Council, was erected in the Market Place in autumn 1908. The main figure behind the project was the best-known Finnish artist of his time, Albert Edelfelt, who had proposed to the council in the 1880's that it should commission a work in bronze from the most distinguished of the Finnish sculptors working in Paris, Ville Vallgren. Vallgren was given a free hand as to the subject, and many rumours were leaked to the press from his atelier in Paris before the work was completed. It was known that it would portray a naked maiden standing on a small rock, having just risen out of the sea, and that she would be ringed by three sea-lions. The sensual female figure was just in the act of turning her head in an attitude of cheeky curiosity, with her chin resting lightly on one hand and the other hand resting on her thigh. It was reported that the decorative base of the statue would represent the vegetation on the sea bed (and some around the mermaid's feet), rocks and codfish and dolphins from which jets of water issued.

The statue was praised as the most beautiful in the Nordic Countries even before it had arrived in Finland, and the Finnish correspondents in Paris described the fountain as "enchantingly intimate", "elegantly harmonious", "monumental" and "stylishly natural". Vallgren's approach to the sculpture was described as inspiringly cheerful: "Die Kunst ist froh". The unveiling of the statue in 1908 led immediately to a division of opinion among the people of Helsinki of such intensity that it became one of the first and most heated controversies over a public work of art to take place in Finland.

There has been much discussion over how the mermaid statue came to be given the name Havis Amanda by the people of Helsinki. Some interpret the young nymph as symbolizing the "new Helsinki" of the future, nurtured by the sea and rising up slowly out of it, while others maintain that it describes the Helsinki of that time, which had already grown up, having first risen from the bosom of the land and sea. When Ville Vallgren himself was asked about this in the 1930's, he replied (whistling snatches of the song "Amanda and Herman") that Havis Amanda is the maiden Amanda of the song, who has just risen up out of the waves, full of health and the joy of life – like Helsinki, which gains its strength and beauty from the waves.

The bold mermaid with her fish and fountains, exuding the joy and light-heartedness of the Paris boulevards, was something new for the Helsinki street scene. Her mischievous nudity set her apart from the nearby statues. The Empress' Stone (C.F. Engel, 1835) in the Market Place, the statue of Runeberg (W. Runeberg, 1885) in the Esplanade Park and the statue of Alexander II (W. Runeberg/J. Takanen, 1894) in the Senate Square, in their classic, masculine solemnity, were all quite different. Havis Amanda reminds us of the time when Finnish artists

were searching for an appropriate ethic and life-style in Paris. Nowadays, she is a symbol of the whole city and is loved by all. It is around her that the First of May is celebrated, the people of the city joining the students in providing the young lady with a student cap, and more recently there have been new variations on this theme. When the Finnish ice hockey team won the World Championships in winter 1995, 100 000 people gathered in the Market Square in Helsinki to celebrate, and Havis Amanda was dressed in an ice hockey shirt.

The Esplanades and the Market Place have maintained their position as important open spaces in the centre of Helsinki. The park has been restored to its former splendour in the last few years, heating has been installed beneath the streets and new shopping centres have been opened, so that those who visit the Esplanades today can truly experience the history of the place and gain a feel of its cultural continuity. The North and South Esplanades are small-scale reflections of the growth of Helsinki from a small Russian town to an urbane business and commercial centre and the modern Finnish city that has been most successful in benefiting from the global economy. The Esplanades, Market Place and South Harbour form the visual and functional core of the city, an impressively harmonious creation of urban architecture. The refurbishing of the Esplanades forms part of a general programme of structural change in Helsinki designed to reinforce its image as a metropolis, and plans are already being laid for a similar restoration of the Market Place.

Havis Amanda, the symbol of Helsinki, was unveiled in the Market Place in autumn 1908. This joyful maiden created by the sculptor Ville Vallgren caused the first controversy over a public monument in Finland.

THE STORY OF THE STATION SQUARE

The majority of the revenues of the Grand Duchy of Finland in the early days went to the building of Helsinki and the transfer and expansion of the University. Then, once the new university buildings had been completed in the mid-1840's, attention was turned to the Saimaa Canal, which, on its completion in 1856, provided the vast waterway systems of Eastern and Central Finland with an outlet to the sea at Vyborg. With the canal functioning, the next in order of priority was the railway. The first railway line, built in 1862, linked Helsinki with the waterways of Häme, allowing access to both water routes and winter roads over the ice. This was followed in 1870 by the main line from Helsinki to St. Petersburg via Vyborg. By that stage Helsinki was connected both with the interior of Finland and, via St. Petersburg, with Moscow, Warsaw, Berlin and all the routes that set out from these centres. Later the long northern branches were to be added, in the directions of Ostrobothnia, Savo and Karelia, together with shorter ones to Turku, Pori and Hanko in the west.

The Finnish railway system pivoted about two points, Helsinki and St. Petersburg. It was only the coming of the railway that gave Helsinki

Helsinki's fine new Railway Station, seen here in the background, was completed just before the First World War, as also was the Kaleva Insurance building on the right. It was to this building that the Seurahuone, the city's oldest and largest hotel and restaurant, was moved.

access to the interior of Finland in an economic sense, leading to the growth of its harbour for exports and particularly for imports. Previous to this Helsinki had mostly been notable for its military garrison, its administrative functions and its university, and had influenced the rest of the country largely in these capacities, but now the growth in commerce and industry meant that it was becoming by far the largest city in the country and a true capital in the commercial sense.

Again we see the decisive role played by government policy and investments in the development of Helsinki. The city had been founded in its time because this was in keeping with the government's general political aims. Vyborg had been built as a matter of general and international policy, but it was Helsinki that had been chosen by the state as the administrative capital of the new Grand Duchy of Finland. Now the railway network, again a government project, was turning it into a commercial centre. Thus Helsinki is not a city which developed as a natural trading point for merchants, an old mercantile town shaped around the civic privileges of the merchant class, but rather a centre that was created and grew up as a specific consequence of government projects.

Helsinki Railway Station was built close to a shallow, boggy bay, Kluuvinlahti, and piles were driven into the bay itself so that this could be converted into an open square. Important public and private buildings were then put up around this square about the turn of the century. The present Railway Station was added just before the First World War, a building of prodigious size and dignified appearance, the work of Eliel Saarinen, Finland's most famous architect after Engel.

Also beside this same square, an impressive building was provided for the *Atheneum* art gallery and the College of Industrial Design in 188. The façade of the *Atheneum* conveys the spirit of conscious identification with European ideals that prevailed in Finland at that time. Early Finnish art and industrial design were based on the models provided by Phidias, Bramante and Rafaello, and alongside their busts, the façade carries mediallions depicting other prominent figures in European art.

Another major cultural edifice was built on the opposite side of the square in 1902, the *National Theatre*, the original Finnish Theatre, which had now adopted this grandiose title. The rough granite mode of expression of its exterior bound it architecturally to nature and prehistory, and in this sense it was the complete antithesis of the Europeanism of the Atheneum. Later the first large statue to the Finnish writer Aleksis Kivi was erected in front of the theatre, the work of the sculptor Wäinö Aaltonen. This meant that the Station Square had

The Station Square is a battleground of European and Finnish national symbolism. The busts of Phidias, Raffaello and Bramante and other ornamentations on the façade of the Atheneum represent Finland's European identity, while the rough-hewn granite and other features of the National Theatre opposite it attempt to be "national" in spirit. In the foreground is a statue of the foremost Finnish-language writer, Aleksis Kivi. The Atheneum links the Station Square with the international element represented by the hotels and restaurants, while the theatre alludes to the connections with the homeland represented by the railway.

gained its own statue of a great man, in the same way as the Senate Square had its monument to Alexander II and the Esplanade its statue of the national poet Runeberg.

Two of the best-known and finest hotels and restaurants in the city, the *Fennia* and the *Seurahuone*, also functioned in the buildings beside the Station Square. The façade of the former carries the names of the main metropolises in Europe, and is in that sense comparable to the Atheneum, while the latter is identifiable with the rough granite tradition of the National Theatre and the Railway Station. Later, in the 1950's, a third well-known hotel rose up on the western edge of the square, the *Vaakuna*, which is linked in its symbolic mode of expression with the nearby functionalist-modernist buildings – only to gain a new neighbour on the other side during the 1990's, Kiasma, The Museum of Contemporary Art, which departs entirely from all previous traditions and represents neither Europeanism nor Finnicism but some notion of Americanism.

The Station Square thus assumed a character of its own in the period between the 1880's and the 1910's, to be followed only a little later by the Hakaniemi Market Place, situated at the north end of Pitkäsilta, the "Long Bridge", at the threshold of the traditional working class residential area. Not far away is the great granite church of Kallio, which binds the area visually with the rest of the city, and the equally granite-dominated façade of the House of the Workers, a monument to the working-class culture of Helsinki and the left-wing political movement, the oldest section of which was built in 1908 and the remainder in 1925. Other buildings that belong inseparably to the world of Hakaniemi are the offices of the trade union organizations and the premises of the old Helsinki cooperative society Elanto.

All the main squares in Helsinki, the Senate Square, the Market Place situated nearby, the Station Square and the Hakaniemi Market have a history that includes traditional markets at which small-scale producers and tradesmen sell their wares. This tradition con-

The former Turuntie
was renamed
Mannerheimintie
to commemorate
Marshal
Mannerheim's 75th
birthday in 1942.
It is literally a road,
"tie", in that it curves
away towards the
north and northwest
independently of the
actual town plan.
This photograph
taken from the tower
of the National
Museum shows the
Hesperia Park on
the right. The Opera
House now stands
on the site marked
by the chimneys
of the old sugar
refinery.

tinues nowadays in the case of Hakaniemi and the Market Place, and both of these have a market hall as well. The Market Place is also famous for its Herring Market that takes place every autumn, when fishermen come in from the islands to sell fish directly from their boats. A further market site close to the city centre is that of Hieta-lahti to the west, which has housed a huge *flea market* since the 1980's. Although bordered on one side by the mighty former main building of the Technical University of Helsinki, this market place has no great monumental or political symbolism behind it. All the others are of some significance as venues for parades, demonstrations and carnevals of one kind or another.

The Senate Square is associated above all with military parades and academic processions, although it is also the site for the annual student torchlight procession on Finnish Independence Day and for welcoming in the New Year. Many very important mass meetings and political demonstrations have also been held there in the course of the last hundred years.

The Market Place is the scene of the May Day festivities, when the students, wearing the white caps that they are awarded on passing their matriculation examinations, flock around Vallgren's *Havis Amanda* fountain, while Hakaniemi has for a long time been a place for political demonstrations and mass meetings, and above all a gathering place for left-wing supporters.

The Station Square has a little of all these traditions, but it is looked on mainly as a *transport* terminal. The Railway Station is there, and the suburban buses leave from there. It is on a main east-west traffic route through the city, the metro runs underneath it. Its north-western edge is marked by the central post office and the large building belonging to the *Sanoma* newspaper and magazine publishers.

On its completion in 1914, the Railway Station building was naturally furnished with a separate entrance and waiting room for the Emperor. Nikolai II managed to use this entrance only once, however, in 1915. Later, the Railway Station was the scene of many important political events, all associated in one way or another with the Soviet Union, starting from the dramatic negotiations in 1939 that ended with the declaration of war. Finnish heads of state would leave for Moscow by train, and Soviet leaders would likewise come to Helsinki by train. The kings of Sweden, on the other hand, have always traditionally arrived by ship, coming ashore at the Market Place.

RESIDENTIAL TÖÖLÖ AND
THE MAIN ROAD NORTH

Signe Brander took photographs of Helsinki in 1908. The first area planning competition in Finland, for the Töölö area, was held in 1898. This rural environment developed into a new suburb of the metropolis within the first decade of the 20th century.

The old residential area of the city of Helsinki is that now known as Kruununhaka, between the Senate Square and the North Shore, after which new housing began to develop to the south and even more obviously to the west. The edges of the city were occupied at first by temporary dwellings and the working class districts. The extreme north of the city area then developed into an industrial zone and a working-class suburb from the mid-19th century onwards, and continued as such for about the next 100 years, until both industry and the new migrants from the countryside began to make for areas further away from the centre. It was through the Hakaniemi Market Place and the northern part of this working-class suburb that the old, his-

Foto Signe Brar

torical *Hämeentie*, the road to Häme, passed on its way to the east and
north. This was one of the two old highways that led out of the city.

The huge new residential area of Töölö grew up at the beginning
of the 20th century in the area north-west of the Station Square, between the bay of Töölönlahti, which projected far into the heart of
the city from the east, and the sea shore to the west of the peninsula. Along the edge of this area ran the second of the ancient thor-
oughfares, the western one, known originally as *Turuntie*, the road to
Turku, and nowadays as *Mannerheimintie*. It is interesting that by contrast
with the very regular layout of the older parts of Helsinki, the two
old roads, *Hämeentie* and *Turuntie*, have preserved their ancient wind-
ing character.

In common with some other towns in Finland, Helsinki named its
main street after Mannerheim, Marshal of Finland, on the occasion of
his 75th birthday in 1942, during the crucial period for the fate of Finland. A statue of him on horseback also stands at an important bend
in this street, at the point where the *Museum of Contemporary Art* was later built. This statue was in fact the first of a series of monuments of a
very diverse nature to be erected in commemoration of the presidents
of Finland: Paasikivi, Svinhufvud, Ståhlberg, Kallio, Ryti and Relan-
der. The strong connection that this area has with the government of
Finland and its statesmen finds its focal point in the fine, dominating
Parliament House, built in 1931, which architecturally represents a dignified classicism and politically sets out to emphasize the sovereignty
and democratic status of the Republic of Finland. It is committed to
the single chamber form of government already decided upon in the
preceding years, and to the system of universal sufferage granted to
Finland by Emperor Nikolai II in 1906.

Before Parliament House, this area of Töölö beside Mannerheimintie had already gained one major building, that of the *National
Museum*. Contrary to the situation in many other countries, the Finnish National Museum is a museum of history, archaeology and eth-
nography rather than of fine art. A later addition to the area has been
Finlandia Hall, a large concert and conference hall complex built in the
1960's, which acquired a position of significance in world history in
1975 as the place where the Conference on Security and Co-opera-
tion in Europe was held. This was the first conference attended by the
heads of state of every one of the European countries, and its resolu-
tions paved the way for the great breakthrough that took place in Europe from 1989 onwards. For the ordinary people of Helsinki, however, this is their much loved concert hall. The city has enjoyed a lively
musical life since the early 19th century, and for a long time this was

The massive Parliament House, dating from 1931 and designed by the architect J.S. Sirén, caused part of the city's governmental life to be moved away from the Senate Square.

Mika Waltari is undoubtedly the best-known internationally of the Finnish writers of the modern era. The students of his own university nation had this monument to him by the sculptor Veikko Hirvimäki erected in 1985.

The building of the National Museum, designed by Herman Gesellius, Armas Lindgren and Eliel Saarinen, was completed in 1906.

The sports stadium, designed by the architects Y. Lindegren and T. Jäntti, was built for the Olympic Games intended to be held in Helsinki in 1940 and was enlarged for the actual games in 1952.

focused on the Great Hall of the University. The new Opera House was also built in this same area on the shore of the bay of Töölönlahti in 1993, emphasizing the role of opera as a highly popular art form both in Helsinki and in Finland as a whole, and one that benefits from considerable government support. In fact, Helsinki must have more in the way of music, theatre and art exhibitions than any other city of its size in the world.

Further out from the city centre is another building of equal importance to Finlandia Hall as far as the history of international relations is concerned, the Olympic Stadium, built originally for the Olympic Games of 1940, which were awarded to Helsinki but were never held, on account of the war. When, in 1952, the games finally came to Finland, the first host country that had been on the losing side in the war, the whole event was of extreme importance as a demonstration of the Finns' national self-esteem, independence and policy of neutrality.

Many large schools form part of the history of Töölö, although some of them have now moved further out into the suburbs, and it also houses the Finnish and Swedish-language schools of economics and business administration and a number of other colleges at various levels. There have been many famous schools in Helsinki as a whole, with traditions that have become a significant part of the history of Finnish thought. Schools play a very important part in the novels of Mika Waltari, a native of Töölö who became one of Finland's most European writers. A widely respected author of historical novels, he possessed a philosophical approach that projected the deep influence of a classical European Latin-based schooling and humanistic academic studies. Waltari is one of those writers whose home town and its young people have chosen to honour with a monument, whereas the masters of fine art and music have not been so fortunate, other than Jean Sibelius, to whom a memorial has been erected in a park in Töölö that bears his name.

THE CITY, ITS SUBURBS AND THE DREAM OF URBAN LIFE

"Helsinki had grown in the course of the years into something that resembled a metropolis. The intensity of the metropolitan bustle had begun to sour its life-style. But the majority of the inhabitants were still small-town folk. They were ready to see an idyll behind every fence that had a green branch leaning over it, and would praise the Lord for every wooden house they passed on their walks."

(Erik Grotenfelt, Bengt Walters' Good Fortune, 1916)

The emergence of the suburb is an essential feature of 19th century European history. Industrialization and the spatial differentiation within towns shed a new light on the problems of urbanization. The writings of both social reformers and urban planners and architects were full of interpretations of the social consequences of industry. The large cities of Europe have indeed demonstrated that the earlier a city became industrialized and began to expand, the more prone it was to social differentiation. Housing shortages in the cities of the 19th century affected both of the "new social classes", the middle class and the working class.

Katajanokka remained on the margins of the city for a long time in the 19th century, a shanty town where the poorer elements lived.

For a long time the situation in Helsinki remained virtually unchanged by European standards, for with the exception of Tampere, industrialization did not serve as a catalyst for urbanization in 19th century Finland in the same way as it did elsewhere in Europe. The majority of the industrial working population continued to live in the countryside up until the last few years of the Grand Duchy period, for it was there that the forest industries grew up, close to the sources of water power, raw materials and good log floating routes. In the case of Helsinki, it may be said that the growth in population was for a long time a matter of an influx of office workers, independent artisans, officials, businessmen, small entrepreneurs, teachers and various categories of service sector employees.

The word "suburb" gained a modern connotation here towards the end of the 19th century as it did elsewhere in Europe: it denoted a dense, urban form of settlement that had established itself beyond the administrative boundary of the town itself, although still within its sphere of influence. Settlement of this kind was common from the 1880's onwards on the fringes of the largest Finnish cities, Helsinki, Vyborg, Turku and Tampere, but the internal hierarchy that it represented was particularly distinct in the case of Helsinki: the areas close to the city centre, symbolically the most important parts, were still inhabited by the upper class, the civil servants and bourgeoisie, while a large number of working class suburban areas grew up in a fairly free, unrestricted manner outside the area of the town plan proper in the 1890's, the best known of which were Hermanni, Pasila, Toukola, Kumpula and Katajanokka. These areas developed a lively urban working class culture, of course, but they were also the focus of all the problems of substandard living conditions and housing shortages.

There was still a serious cultural, political and mental boundary in the Finland of the turn of the century that divided the towns from the countryside, and although the "gentlefolk" and the "common people" pursued very different life-styles in the towns, it was still common in Helsinki to find different social groups living in the same building and sharing the same yard, the upper class in the best apartments and the working class people in the outbuildings, attics and basements. Nor was there yet any boundary between the city and its suburbs at the turn of the century. Even so, little could be done about the uncontrolled growth of urban settlement in Helsinki, any more than in other large European cities, and the shortage of housing, which had persisted since the 1850's, became one of the most pressing political issues.

The principal psychological and ideological rationale behind the development of suburbs nevertheless lay in mastery over the fear

The Senate Square became the main venue for political demonstrations at the beginning of the 20th century. This picture taken in front of the Senate building conveys the atmosphere during the year of the General Strike, 1905. The building in the centre, the Sederholm House (1757), is the oldest surviving stone-built house in Helsinki.

of town life. In the case of Helsinki the tension between urbanization and suburbanization came to a head in 1906–1908. Although noises of a new form of political activation had reverberated from Paris and from the continent originally in connection with the uprising of 1848, the political awakening of the working classes occurred very suddenly in Finland, and with unprecedented violence, in 1905–1906. The General Strike and the Sveaborg mutiny served to shape middle class opinion instantly and very radically. The emergence of the working class as a political force in the large cities throughout Europe brought to the forefront the question of what should be done to exercise social control and preserve the legally constituted social order. The gulf created in society by the rising working class was equally visible in London, Berlin or Paris as it was in Stockholm or St. Petersburg, in the form of attempts by the urban leadership to protect and defend their position. The awakening of the upper classes and intellectuals to this world of political class distinctions proceeded under more or less the same banners in Helsinki as it did in the other cities of Western Europe. The problems raised by rapid, uncontrolled urban growth paved the way for a mood of revulsion towards urban life in general from the 1880's onwards. The antithesis of the violent, dirty, dangerous city was an idyllic, harmonious, aesthetically inspiring pre-industrial environment, the physical symbols of which were nature, light, air, space and greenness. The pan-European roots of the fear of towns lay in this escapist attitude towards urban reality, which then assumed particular, national forms in each country.

The change in attitudes took place relatively late in Finland by European standards, and it was only the political upheavals of the early years of the 20th century that introduced the notion of a fear of towns into the vocabulary of middle and upper class Helsinki. The resulting formation of land holding companies, chiefly a response to the general European cultural trend of "Away from the evils of the town!", was admittedly partly inspired by the shortage of building land in Helsinki, a problem that affected all sectors of society. It was believed, again in the European mould, that the political uncertainty could be eliminated by means of environmental reforms and the construction of better living surroundings than prevailed at the time. A beautiful suburban atmosphere would inevitably have a social impact, creating more contented people, a more harmonious family life and a more peaceful society.

As awareness of the nature of urban dwelling grew, it became possible to demonstrate that the causes and consequences of many of the problems afflicting society were to be found in rapid, uncontrolled urbanization. Mortality was higher in the towns than in the countryside, poor food, deficient hygiene and inadequate water supplies, sewerage and waste disposal encouraged the spread of serious diseases such as tuberculosis and cholera, and alcoholism, prostitution and the abandonment of children were specifically urban phenomena, as were the strikes, demonstrations, anarchy in the streets and political violence that had been brought about by the organized working class. In accordance with thinking in the natural sciences of the day, environmental factors were seen as affecting people's human and biological evolution.

This abhorrence of towns inspired a romantic view of what was a good living environment. Where "evil" was equated with a bad, cramped urban environment, a suburban, putatively rural, spacious, light, garden-like environment came to represent everything that was "good". A close, organic relationship with nature, the landscape and the countryside was looked on as an instrument for achieving good, edifying, non-violent social reform. It was on these assumptions that the metropolises of Europe began to gain suburban belts of middle and upper class villas in the 19th and 20th centuries. Spacious housing estates of this kind developed towards the end of the 19th century in places such as Essen in Germany and Birmingham and Liverpool in Britain as the industrial magnates sought to build idyllic, garden suburbs for their staff and workers. The book *Tomorrow, a Peaceful Path to Real Reform*, in which the English social reformer Ebenezer Howard set out his ideas on the combining of the advantages of both urban and rural dwelling in the form of an independent, self-sufficient *garden city*, spread around the world and was well known in Finland.

Russian tourism and the summer villas favoured by the upper class and merchants had given rise to extensive areas of superior housing on the outskirts of Helsinki by the latter half of the 19th century, but it was only with the greater upheaval in the social system and the growth in middle class power and influence that living in villas and detached houses all the year round became common practice. The great suburban breakthrough took place in Helsinki in 1905–1906, at the time when the first mass working class demonstrations and attempted uprisings politicised the whole social climate, simultaneously intensifying the mood of disgust with town life. General public opinion was imbued with a fear of the consequences of working class unrest.

Private initiatives led to the creation of a number of land holding companies in the parish of Helsinge and the rural district of Espoo in the years 1905–1908, for the purpose of constructing modern communities of villas and detached houses in spacious, green surroundings for the use of middle class and better-off working class families. This may be looked on as one consequence of social change, the first extensive attempt at intervening to solve the worst of the city's problems, the shortage of housing and building land for all classes in society.

This form of company had two ideas behind it: it was a means of reacting quickly and appropriately to the challenges of modern planning and building, and it was a convenient combination of capital, land acquisition and the implementation of an extensive programme of new building. Also, the introduction of the corporate principle into urban building served as an indirect indication that planning in Helsinki was felt to be an excessively centralized, inflexible affair. Certainly it had been very slow to react to the new demands placed on the urban environment at the beginning of the century.

The land holding companies and the garden suburbs built on their initiative in the Kulosaari, Kauniainen, Haaga, Lauttasaari, Munk-kiniemi, Tapaninkylä and Pukinmäki areas represented a combination of the most up-to-date knowledge of planning and construction with superior financial expertise. Building took place in these areas on the strength of private capital and enterprise. The urban objectives as such were largely shaped by architects and engineers, united by a common vision of what constituted a good, modern urban structure, while capital was provided by bankers, merchants and businessmen who were interested in building projects. This new building elite emerged in Finland at a time when the society of the estates was just undergoing transformation into a class society. Initiative, individuality and enterprise were the hallmarks of the new urban elite, offering a distinct alternative to the centrally managed building tradition led by the officials and the way of life in which each person was conscious of his or her own social standing.

The elegant suburbs and the well designed homes – whether villas or detached houses – had a distinct social purpose behind them. It was necessary to create better urban people, to support the integrity

Private detached houses and villas spread to Helsinki with the creation of the suburbs. This advertisement put about by a land holding company in 1910 emphasizes closeness to nature and individuality.

of family life and to ensure welfare and continuity in society. Housing and the suburban environment became crucial instruments in the struggle against the detrimental consequences of urbanization. The green suburbs and the detached houses that they contained soon gained an established position in Helsinki, and ownership of the land that one's home stood on came to be regarded as the best guarantee of peace in the community.

If suburban life gained support from an abhorrence of towns, then the semi-urban Finnish landscape ideal and the foundation for the new urban identity sprang up from precisely these roots. Thus the fear of towns gave rise in the course of the second decade of the new century to a parallel phenomenon in the bourgeois trend in literature, a more gloomy, pessimistic view of towns, and particularly of Helsinki. The main theme was once more the attractions of the town, the opportunity for greater affluence and a continental life-style in contrast to the demoralizing personal effects of urban life. The towns tempted people with "the music of sirens" in order to plunge them to their doom, as L. Onerva described it in her collection of short stories entitled *Nousukkaita*, "The Upstarts" (1911). Similarly, Eino Leino's *Pankkiherroja*, "Gentlemen of the Bank" (1914) offers us a delightful picture of the dynamics of this rise and fall, of the Helsinki world of financial success, speculation and bankruptcy.

The middle class garden suburbs lay beyond the administrative boundaries of Helsinki itself, in the rural districts, with their predominantly agrarian way of life, where building could go on in a fairly free and uncontrolled manner. The presence of many distinguished architects among the shareholders in the land holding companies meant that certain private land use plans such as that devised by Eliel Saarinen for Munkkiniemi and Haaga and that of Bertel Jung for the island of Kulosaari became internationally acclaimed classics of urban planning in that decade. The first journal of town planning to be published in Finland was in fact *Brändö Meddelanden*, "Kulosaari Communications", a few issues of which were produced there in 1917.

The people who had houses built in the garden suburbs and estates in effect defined a new attitude towards urban structure for the early years of the century, creating the foundation for an urban reality that appeals to and unites different generations of Helsinki dwellers even today. The suburb, a European innovation familiar from the great metropolises, was a conjunction of the landscape ideal and unspoiled nature of a rural district with the opportunities opened up by an urbane way of life. This combination is still patent a hundred years later. The urban culture of Helsinki is still powered by its sub-

Private land holding companies were set up at the beginning of the 20th century to build the first garden suburbs, a trend which was greatly promoted by the emergence of modern urban planning. The picture shows Eliel Saarinen's plan of 1915 for the Munkkiniemi-Haaga area, which already contains a premonition of the future expansion of the city.

urbs and outlying districts, just as the collective memory binds the true Finnish character to nature and the values and traditions of the countryside.

The predominance of small detached houses, the closeness to nature, the exploitation of the landscape and terrain, and the uniformity and intimacy of the private communities of villas in the immediate vicinity of Helsinki were elements and symbols of a new kind in urban planning, departing markedly from the earlier tradition of urban structure in Helsinki. It is no coincidence that the plans for these communities were conceived at a time when the deficiencies inherent in the old centralized disposition of the city were coming to the fore. The aim, as the new generation of community-oriented architects that emerged at the beginning of the century were anxious to point out, was to replace the centralized, rational, measured, monumental, ponderous, regular forms that had dominated the art of designing the disposition of a city with a picturesque, irregular system.

More indirectly, the aim was to break down the century-old, powerful presence of the state within the capital. The creation of the suburbs was the first residents' movement to affect the affairs of the city, a reaction to the nature of state authority and the urban structures and aesthetic values that reproduced that authority. The Helsinki of the 19th century had become a symbol of Finland's constitutional existence, a functional and political platform for the exercise of government. The city had been a building project consciously intended to emphasize its own status as the nation's capital. Its squares, streets, houses and parks had been designed to meet the requirements of formality. "Helsinki truly has never been anything more than public buildings and a few rare private dwelling houses left in the centre as relics of Swedish times", Zachris Topelius wrote of the city of his youth in the 1880's, and went on, "One Swedish traveller who came to the city over land remarked that 'it is no more than barracks and hospitals', while a Russian who arrived by sea commented 'Schöne Aussenseite und nichts dahinten'". Long, broad streets and wide squares are sequences of hyphens that lead off into the unknown future, as Topelius put it, "But what in our day we call community spirit and the life of the people, that was something that the command from on high was quite incapable of conjuring suddenly out of the egg of the little town as it was then. Finland's new capital city was still in just as immature a state in the 1830's as Jeppe Nilsson waking up to find himself an aristocratic gentleman."

The pioneers of the suburbs set out to break down the centrality inherited from the times of King Gustavus Vasa that had created the urban spirit of the Finnish towns. It was by nature a spirit that emphasized regularity, an inorganic, hierarchical spirit that frequently served to underline the functions of the supreme power. It was the antithesis of the freedom of the peasant farmers and the independent way of life of the villages that prevailed in Finland and Sweden. The great self-confidence of the builders of the Helsinki villas was grounded in pre-industrial peasant notions of self-sufficiency and in admiration for the medieval concept of the town. Unfortunately the social climate of the post-1918 capital left little room for these values and ideals.

May 1917 was a time of splendid celebrations in the garden city of Kulosaari, still part of the rural district of Helsinge at that stage. It was the 10th anniversary of the local land holding company, Ab Brändö Villastad. A portrait of the "Pioneers of Brändö" by a local artist, Wilho Sjöström, was unveiled, and a history in rhymed couplets (Sw. nidvisa) of the ten founders of the community and the early stages of its existence, composed by the architect Bertel Jung, was recited. The atmosphere was one of great nostalgic satisfaction. Within those ten years some of the most brilliant of the capital's new middle class, liberal business elite had been instrumental in creating a modern suburb. The company was the biggest landowner in the metropolitan area in 1917, and had new building plans extending as far as Porvoo.

The enthusiasm of the designers and builders of Kulosaari and their sense of enterprise even under urban conditions opened up exceptional prospects. They looked upon themselves as urban pioneer

This scene on the island of Kulosaari in 1910 serves well to indicate what features were emphasized in a modern garden suburb. The idyll is filled out by the presence of modern technology in the form of the telephone and electricity wires and the tram connection with the city centre.

settlers, *conditores urbis*. Finnish pioneers have traditionally been responsible for the settlement of the countryside, struggling to conquer the boggy outback, but a pioneering, enterprising spirit has been a rarer thing in the towns. Unfortunately, in spite of the promising beginning, these pioneers of suburban dwelling never rose to the status of a cultural model for the Finns. The image of the diligent, hard-working, flaxen-haired Finn in his rough woollen shirt cursing as he cleared the forest to create fields has clung on tenaciously in the national consciousness. The Finns are eternally suspicious of the education and urban way of life that a city represents.

It was nevertheless the case that the private land holding companies were the largest landowners in the metropolitan area before 1917, as the machinery of the local authority itself was not yet geared to acquiring land. There was in fact little support in administrative circles for public sector land ownership, especially as it would have been incompatible with the policy espoused by the local leadership, who looked on any extension of the city as a source of new expenditure on roads, water supplies, lighting and the maintenance of law and order, etc. Thus when Helsinki City Council had been offered the opportunity to purchase the islands of Lauttasaari and Kulosaari in 1911–1912 it had declined: its leaders were not interested in expansion either eastwards or westwards!

The consequence of this was that the new suburban communities remained legislatively, judicially and administratively inaccessible to the City Council and were able to develop in a free and unrestrained manner – for good or ill. Similarly the local authorities of the rural district of Espoo and the parish of Helsinge showed no interest in supervising these communities. This indeterminate situation meant that the suburbs were able to exist as self-governing areas or built-up communities. The legislative reform of 1919 then allowed such a community to become a borough or rural district if the majority of its inhabitants so wished.

Movements in this direction were made all the more probable by the unstable local government situation in the rural districts of Espoo and Helsinge, and the first new local authorities to be created, by a Senate decision of 1921, were thus the rural districts of Haaga-Huopalahti and Oulunkylä (Haaga becoming a borough in its own right in 1922). The unanimous support of the inhabitants for this solution was ascertained in the case of Huopalahti in what was probably the only local referendum of its kind ever to be held in Finland. The garden city of Kulosaari began life as a rural district on 1.1.1922.

Times and customs change, however, and the social tensions of 1917–1918 altered the visions entertained by the builders overnight. The immediate outcome was the collapse of private building and an increasing mutual dependence between the city of Helsinki and its surrounding local authorities in the course of the 1920's. At the same time the City Council began to adopt a more positive land acquisition policy and to purchase shares in the land holding companies that had built the suburban estates. A new understanding of local authority finances came to the fore in which Helsinki and its surroundings were viewed as a single economic region and it was realized that growth of the metropolitan area called for centralized administration. The turning point was the passing of a law in 1925 that enabled the existing local government boundaries in the area to be altered if they led to unsatisfactory conditions in the suburbs.

The rise and fall of private suburban building in Helsinki should be viewed as part of the Finnish political and social reality of the day. The middle-class, liberal, urban spirit of private enterprise and political activity grounded in this were not allowed to squeeze themselves to the forefront of attention, even though capital had begun to accumulate in Helsinki and the other major coastal and industrial towns as long ago as the 1860's.

The time was ripe for urbanization on the European model and the development of the city according to the interests of the inhabitants themselves. But although the change was a significant one, its influence was more tenuous on a national scale. The extent of the middle class and of the wealth possessed by it remained well below the level to be found in other European capitals. The reasons for this lay in the social structure of the country as a whole. Even in 1870 only 7.5% of the Finnish population were living in the towns, one of the lowest proportions to be found anywhere in Europe, and the population of Helsinki had not yet passed the 35 000 mark.

The crucial question for the Helsinki pioneers at the beginning of the 20th century was whether Finland could be fashioned into a modern European state that was reliant on the vitality of its towns and cities. At the same time the key positions in the task of defining the new national image were held not by the new middle class but by the academic circle of intellectuals and the rising working class. It was the former that defined the nation's attitude towards Finnish identity at the end of the 19th century, and there was no place in this identity for an urban culture. The politics of the Fennomans in the latter half of the 19th century had laid emphasis on the connection between the urban intellectuals and the peasant ethos of the countryside, with the

Helsinki is a city of innumerable parks. This is a view of the park on the slopes of the Observatory Hill in the late 1910's.

greater accent on the latter, and the schism between the Fennomans and the liberals towards the end of that period, as the new urban and industrial Finland was beginning to emerge, had been resolved in favour of the Fennomans for the time being. Liberalism, the ideology of merchants, industrialists, businessmen and artisans all over Europe in the last century, remained a somewhat marginal phenomenon in Finland, as the formation of political parties here was strongly influenced by the question of language.

The strengthening of the national identity was a consequence of the cultural and educational work carried out amongst ordinary people in the provinces and the countryside. A powerful state and a well functioning provincial organization served as guarantees of internal unity. On the other hand, the material and moral inadequacies brought about by the growth of the towns were reflected in literature and the arts, with writers who had adopted a working-class ideology focusing attention on the living conditions of the urban and industrial working population. Critical attitudes came to a head from time to time in actual condemnations. Some of the novels and vignettes branded the metropolis as "the most devilish invention in the world", the creators of which, the architects and master builders, "should be hung from the same gallows as the landladies of cheap boarding houses". Thus it must be admitted that the Finland of the modern, liberal, industrial cities on the coast, the Finland of navigation and commerce, was left in the minority in the act of defining the national and cultural ethos in the early 20th century. The Finnish city and the Finnish city dweller never at any stage reached the forefront as an instrument of identification as was the case on the continent, where urban man, his achievements and his military, industrial and economic initiative, particularly in the colonies, occupied a prominent position in

One application of the notion of a garden city in Helsinki is the wooden-built district of Käpylä. This was one of the most significant concentrations of working-class housing in Finland in the 1920's.

society and in the national self-image. Instead, it was the lakes, hills and unspoiled forests that formed the dominant image, one derived from the interior of Finland. The harshness of nature and the ruggedness of the landscape were looked on as having left their impression on the Finnish mentality, a mentality which scarcely had any points of contact with urban reality or the culture of the cities.

The absence of an urban identity was also evident in the spectrum of political parties as it was a hundred years ago, in that Finland still lacked a party that represented the merchants and urban middle class. Urban liberalism was in practice suppressed beneath a rural outlook on life that had come to dominate the party ideologies of the turn of the century. Most of the major class-based parties in Finland, such as the Agrarian Party or the Social Democrats, have from the outset been concerned over the consequences of urbanization and the abandonment of the countryside, and although the Swedish People's Party originally defined its support on linguistic grounds, it soon found itself reliant on the Swedish-speaking farmers and fishermen of the coastal regions. The directions that political parties were to take were to a great extent dictated by the voters, whose background remained predominantly rural, as the SDP was soon to find out, for although its roots lay in the international outlook and working class values inherent in urban life, it obtained the majority of its votes at the beginning of the century from the tenant farmers and landless population in the countryside. Similarly, the successors of the Fennoman parties, the Coalition Party and the National Progressive Party, both retained a certain "peasant ideology" for a long time.

The Finnish urban mentality at the turn of the century was the outcome of a multi-level process of social change that had attached a strong sense of urban phobia to our notions of the city and its way of life. It was at this same period that the Finnish political identity also took shape, largely on the strength of a national culture that contained ingredients from Fennomania, the agrarian and rural idealism of the peasant state, the symbolism of the forests and the romanticism of the *Kalevala*. In time, the bipolarization into a rural Finland and an administrative Finland of power and influence had a deep-seated effect on the national self-image, and it meant that emphasis on urban culture remained for a long time a marginal and largely Helsinki-centred affair.

As noted above, the cause of the urban community was not advanced by Finland's gaining independence nor by the events of 1918. The timbers from which the national identity of the young republic was constructed still grew in the landscapes of Topelius and the human ideals of Runeberg. Myths and legends were created around the peasant army of the Whites during the Civil War and the rural basis of the new national unity. There was no room in the new, independent Finland for the private enterprise represented by the suburban land holding companies, nor was the capital anywhere to be found. The focus of political and juridical ingenuity in the young republic was on solving the problems of the rural proletariat, the tenant farmers, or crofters, and on working towards national unity. The main achievement in the early stage of independence was the formation of a large class of small farmers whose ownership of the land would guarantee national continuity and a foundation for the state. Liberation of the crofters and the formation of an independent farming population were the chief methods adopted in the internal confrontation between the Finland of the middle classes and the Finland of the socialists, and the role of Helsinki in this game remained a negligible one.

Although the majority of present-day Finns live in urban surroundings, discussions have returned in recent times to the topic of the dichotomy between urban dwelling and a suburban life close to nature. The concept of Nurmijärvi living was coined in political circles in the very first years of the new millennium to give expression to this ideal (Nurmijärvi is an independent municipality with many features of a rural environment on the fringe of the metropolitan area of Helsinki), and the discussion came to be focused on the requirements for good living in the Helsinki area and the need for urban expansion. It is still possible to see over and over again how people migrating to the area find a new home for themselves and the key to urban living from somewhere in between the two extreme types of model community that the district has to offer: the natural surroundings of Kulosaari or Nurmijärvi and the urban milieu of Töölö or Ruoholahti. The situation will remain unique by European standards all the time the majority of us are still in the process of becoming city dwellers and learning to appreciate the advantages of urban life.

Helsinki has proved to be a melting pot for the Finns and their concepts of national identity. Those who come here are mostly young men and women, of working age and intent on studying further. And nowadays very many of them are coming alone, so that almost half the households in the city itself consist of a single person only, a proportion that has doubled over the last 25 years. They are supported in their independence and self-reliance by the fact that Helsinki continues to have an abundance of accommodation for small households, as over half the apartments in the city are of one or two rooms. At the same time families are moving out into the suburbs in search of better living conditions in places where they can build new houses for themselves more cheaply, according to their own tastes, and live closer to nature. These two extremes in ideal Finnish landscapes are destined to compete with each other for a long time into the future!

The pattern of alliances that eventually determined the course of the First World War began to emerge from 1888 onwards and assumed concrete form in 1893, when Russia and France formed a military alliance directed against the rapidly increasing might of a Germany united under the Kaiser. When Germany then began to develop a powerful navy in the late 1890's, mostly based at Kiel on the Baltic Sea, Russia also set about renewing its naval capability and reinforcing its long Baltic coast, which extended at that time from Tornio in the north to the boundary with East Prussia close to Königsberg (present-day Kaliningrad) in the south. When the First World War finally broke out the German fleet was mostly engaged in combat with the British navy, but it was still by no means certain in the 1890's that Britain would join the anti-German front, since that country was a competitor and enemy of Russia in Asia and a competitor and enemy of France

Advertisement in Russian, Finnish and Swedish for a performance of a French operetta at the Alexander Theatre in aid of the Russian Red Cross during the First World War.

in Africa. All this meant that the German naval build-up was directed far more obviously against Russia than the actual events of the war would give one to believe.

This being the case, Russia was obliged to look after the defences of the long coastline of Finland. The Diet of the four estates was nevertheless sharply opposed to any extension to Finland of the system of compulsory military service that applied elsewhere in the Russian Empire, and the consequence, after six years of conflict, was the abolition of the separate body of Finnish troops. From that time onwards the Grand Duchy of Finland made its own defence contribution in the form of monetary payments. There had been a certain Russian military presence continuous at Sveaborg and in various other places, and on the eve of the First World War it was indeed the case that Finland had only Russian troops to defend it. These Russian troops were on the whole on fairly good terms with the Finnish civilian population, in addition to which, following the old custom, there were many Finns serving as officers in various parts of the Russian Empire, including some who took part in the Russo-Japanese War of 1904–1905.

It was the disagreement over compulsory military service that ushered in the period of mass political demonstrations in Helsinki. The first conscriptions, in March 1902, led to protest meetings in the Senate Square, at which the Russian troops – the feared Cossacks –

Vast fortifications were constructed around Helsinki during the First World War, both on the outer islands and on the landward side. The coastal artillery, searchlights, storehouses and everything else gave an impression of being new and extremely efficient. The city was ringed on its land side with a chain of trenches and bunkers. The Germans never attempted to invade, however.

contented themselves with the minimum measures possible, as the Tsar did not want to aggravate the situation. These demonstrations had been the work of the right wing, but this political mobilization of the people was to turn against the upper classes when defeat in the war with Japan led to a general period of unrest throughout Russia in 1905, as the outcome in Helsinki and in Finland in general, as elsewhere, was a *general strike* in November 1905, with political gatherings in the Station Square: the situation came very close to an armed encounter between the marshals acting for the Whites and Reds. An armed conflict did in fact ensue the following summer in the Hakaniemi Square, when some of the working people of Helsinki went on strike again in support of the large-scale mutiny among the sailors stationed at Sveaborg. Political life in Finland was centred on Helsinki and its market squares, and was closely bound up with events in Russia and in the world at large.

As the World War approached, and even after it had broken out, work went on to construct the huge *Peter the Great Marine Barrier* on both sides of the Gulf of Finland, in Helsinki and Tallinn, for the purpose of closing off the gulf and protecting St. Petersburg. This new project, comparable in size to the building of Sveaborg, meant the construction of fortifications on many of the outer islands off Helsinki and the arming of these with modern coastal defence artillery and gigantic floodlight systems. It also meant the building of a very extensive series of land fortifications around Helsinki (and correspondingly around Tallinn) to prevent the enemy from attacking these systems from the rear. Defence installations were also put into position on the west coast of Finland and a defence line developed across Finland itself – since Sweden was known to be favourably disposed towards Germany and might very well join the war on the other side.

The *Peter the Great Marine Barrier* and most of the Russian *Baltic Fleet*, which remained in Helsinki throughout the war, never came under fire at all, as the war between Russia and Germany was conducted on land, the fronts being located in Poland, Livonia and Rumania. The fleet was kept on the alert, but was never in action, which naturally led to frustration and the spread of revolutionary ideas. The revolution of March 1917 in Russia did in fact lead to mutinies and the murder of officers in Helsinki and Sveaborg. At the same time it meant the end of the favourable course of the war as far as Finland was concerned, and the cessation of work on the fortifications, which had been a source of easy income for many people. The men released from the fortification work now became the crucial nucleus of the Red Guards. Signs of anarchy were to be seen in Finland as well during the summer of 1917, and the country went through a general strike and a state of *Red Terror* in the course of the autumn, when factory managers, estate owners and other "bourgeois" were executed. This in turn led the upper classes to form *Civil Guard* detachments.

When the Bolsheviks seized power in St. Petersburg at the beginning of November 1917, the constitutional bond between the Grand Duchy of Finland and Russia was broken, and Parliament declared Finland an independent state on 6th December 1917. Russia under Lenin, followed by France, Sweden, Germany, Austria-Hungary and many other countries had formally recognized Finland by 4.1.1918, but there were still large numbers of Russian troops in the country and the internal situation was extremely unstable. This culminated in a war of independence, or Civil War, that broke out at the end of the same month.

German soldiers in front of the Hotel Kämp in Helsinki in April 1918. The Germans' Baltic Division landed at Hanko and occupied Helsinki, where a Soviet-inspired revolution had taken place in January. The revolutionary government of the Reds fled the city and the legal government gradually returned to its former duties.

93

At the same time as the government fled from Helsinki, established a bridgehead of the *Whites* in Ostrobothnia and began to disarm the Russian troops there, the socialists and Red Guards took control of the capital and declared a People's Republic of Finland. The war gained momentum at the beginning of March, when the government asked Imperial Germany to intervene (there were already German troops in Estonia), and the White army under the command of General Mannerheim was in a hurry to gain a decisive victory before the Germans arrived. Mannerheim did in fact succeed in capturing the city of Tampere from the Reds, although with heavy losses of lives, but it was the Germans, who had landed at Hanko at about the same time, who regained control over Helsinki.

The Baltic Division of the Imperial German Army marched into Helsinki under the command of their general, Count von der Goltz, on 12th–14th April, at which time the Red revolutionaries fled to the east. Soon after this the German naval squadrons arrived. The upper classes in Helsinki went through a phase of eager Germanophilia at this time, the foundation for which had been laid by the anxiety over the spread of anarchism and revolutionary ideologies and over the dangers of Red Terror which had begun in 1905 and increased greatly in 1917. This new trend met with especially strong support in the Swedophile sector of the community both in Helsinki and in the country at large, so that the former linguistic dichotomy between the pro-Finnish and pro-Swedish factions took on racialist tones that were typical of the spirit of the age. The influence of universal suffrage and the growing support for socialism had aroused fears that were then inflamed by the Red Terror of 1917 and events in the Baltic States.

Mannerheim was nevertheless opposed to the Germans and trusted in eventual victory for France, Britain and the Russian Whites. In order to make an impression on the Germanophiles of Helsinki, he therefore arranged a great parade of his "peasant army" on 16th May 1918, a symbolic gesture that had the effect of linking the sovereignty now gained by Finland with the ancient patriotic tradition as conceived by Runeberg in his time. Mannerheim even chose to review his troops in front of the statue of Runeberg – and then left the country in protest at the influence accorded to the Germans.

The tragic last act of the Civil War consisted of the concentration camps in which the Red Guard prisoners were detained, since the government did not dare to let them free at once under the existing circumstances. Starvation and disease in these camps claimed the lives of thousands during the summer of 1918. One such camp was located at Sveaborg.

Cavalry General G. Mannerheim reviewed a march-past of troops of the Whites on 16th May 1918 in front of the statue of the national poet, Runeberg. Mannerheim wished in this way to emphasize the part played by the Finnish troops in winning the war for the Whites and to prevent Imperial Germany from gaining too strong an influence in Finland.

The World War having ended in defeat for Germany, the German troops left Helsinki at the end of 1918, and Mannerheim returned from abroad to act as Regent of Finland for the spring and summer of 1919. In July of that year he signed the Finnish Constitution, which remained in force until the year 2000. Its concept of the concentration of power in the president followed a tradition going back to the 18th century and proved its worth most obviously during the long period after the Second World War when successful management of relations with the Soviet Union called for great skill and concentration of efforts.

Military and Civil Guard parades were commonplace in the Helsinki of the 1920's and 1930's, and they reappeared from the 1960's

President Urho Kekkonen unveiled a handsome statue of Mannerheim on horseback, the work of Aimo Tukiainen, beside Mannerheimintie in 1960. The national campaign to raise money for the statue was in itself a major expression of political will, especially since a great deal of money was left over. The unveiling ceremony and its march-past was also an outstanding occasion. The photograph shows the flags of the war veterans and students with their white caps.

onwards. In common with the general trend in Europe, there was even a "peasant march" on Helsinki in 1930, although in this case it did not lead to any change in the system of government.

When Baron Gustaf Mannerheim, Marshal of Finland, died in January 1951, his lying in state in the Church of St. Nicholas in Helsinki and his funeral cortège on an exceptionally cold February day constituted a massive display of patriotism. A national collection to cover the cost of his statue yielded funds far in excess of those required, and the resulting statue was duly unveiled by President Kekkonen on Mannerheim's birthday, 4th June 1960.

HELSINKI IN THE SECOND
WORLD WAR

When the French and British negotiators returned home from Moscow in August 1939 via Helsinki, their joint statement made it clear that in their opinion there were difficult times ahead for Finland. Germany and the Soviet Union had signed a non-aggression pact on 23.8.1939 and had secretly agreed to a division of the countries located between their territories, including Finland, into spheres of interest. The war itself began on 1st September 1939, when Germany invaded Poland, two days later France and Britain had declared war on Germany, and two weeks later the Soviet Union attacked Poland. Finland immediately declared her neutrality and recalled the most recently discharged national servicemen to strengthen the defence of this neutrality.

At the end of September Estonia handed over certain areas of its territory only about 100 km away from Helsinki to the Soviet Union for the establishment of military bases, and similar territorial demands were made of Latvia and Lithuania, to which they acceded. In October 1939 the Soviet Foreign Minister Molotov proposed negotiations with Finland in Moscow over granting the Soviet Union the use of various parts of the Gulf of Finland, the Hanko Peninsula and the Karelian Isthmus, on the grounds of the need to secure the defences of Leningrad. Finland began taking precautionary measures, and its regular army was placed on a defensive alert. The Finnish White Guards were dispatched to the Isthmus and the Uusimaa Regiment to Hanko, both at wartime battalion strength. Full mobilization came into force in Helsinki in mid-October, slightly later than elsewhere in the country, for reasons of caution.

During October long military trains transported the 4th Division, formed by troops from the Uusimaa Military Province, to the Karelian Isthmus. The majority of the Finnish-speaking reservists from Helsinki served in the 11th Infantry Regiment and their Swedish-speaking counterparts in the 10th Infantry Regiment. The 11th Infantry Regiment became one of the best-known army units in the course of the war, and was renowned for its spirit of comradeship. It was a regiment in which men from all branches of society fought side by side: carpenters and teachers, managers and unskilled labourers.

At the same time as the Finnish negotiators, Paasikivi and Tanner, set out for Moscow in October, the voluntary evacuation of Helsinki began. The city prepared to face air attacks, which meant that the schools were closed and the air-raid shelters were reinforced. The armaments, ammunition and explosives factories were moved to safer sites outside the city. The people of Helsinki were given instructions on what to do in the case of air raids, and trenches were dug in the parks.

Negotiations in Moscow were broken off on 14th November 1939, and 14 days later the Soviet Union abrogated its non-aggression treaty with Finland. The war began on 30th November, when Soviet troops crossed the border of Finland. An air attack began at dawn and the first air-raid warning was sounded in Helsinki at 9.16 a.m. The bombing continued for two days. The Bus Station, the Technical University and a number of other buildings in the city centre were hit, and one apartment building collapsed entirely. People moving about in the streets were shot at with rifles from the aircraft as they flew over. In December the weather became sufficiently bad that the enemy air attacks were interrupted for a few days, which made it easier to move people away from the capital.

This first period of bombing was in fact the worst of the whole Winter War. Altogether 91 people were killed and 236 injured. It was calculated that the enemy aircraft had dropped a total of 133 explosive bombs and 60 incendiary bombs. Further smaller air raids were made in December and January, but the Russian navy never came near Helsinki at any stage. It has often been asked why the Soviet Union spared the city. Air-raid warnings were sounded on 81 occasions in the course of the Winter War, and the periods of alert lasted for a total of 73 hours, but the city was actually bombed only nine times, whereas the very much smaller town of Hanko in Uusimaa had to cope with as many as 72 air attacks.

On the outbreak of war, President Kallio handed over the command of the military forces to Marshal Mannerheim, who set up his headquarters in the city for a short time, using some of the sturdily built hotels, before moving it to Mikkeli for the duration of the war. In spite of the war, an Independence Day reception was arranged at the Hotel Kämp. The President lived on the island of Kuusisaari throughout the Winter War, and the cabinet met in the air-raid shelter beneath the Bank of Finland building. The Ministry of Defence moved to refurbished underground premises tunnelled into the rock in the Meilahti area that had also been used for this purpose during the First World

Splinter protection on the wall of the Police Offices in October 1939, during the Winter War. In the background are the Senate Square and the city's most prominent symbol, the Church of St. Nicholas, nowadays Helsinki Cathedral.

The foreign war correspondents made themselves at home in the bar of the Hotel Kämp, which had been converted into an air raid shelter.

War, and into some nearby villas. Parliament was transferred all the way to Kauhajoki in Ostrobothnia.

Each morning the people of Helsinki would look out of their windows to see what the weather was like. A beautiful clear morning was an immediate threat, whereas mist or rain was more reassuring, and snow was the sign of a peaceful day. The Russians flew during the daylight hours, and usually approached Helsinki from the sea, seldom from inland. The people quickly learned to recognise the repeated rising and falling tones of the air defence sirens, and would hurry into the cellars of their own buildings or into a public air-raid shelter such as a trench in a park or shelter cut into the rock. The "All Clear" was a long, continuous level tone.

The struggle mounted by the Finns against overwhelming odds aroused great sympathy throughout the world. Large numbers of foreign correspondents arrived in Helsinki, and most of them stayed in the Hotel Kämp in the

Esplanade. The majority of the townspeople remained in their homes in spite of the danger and tried to carry on normal lives. The windows of the dwellings were blacked out and the street lamps were put out completely when an air-raid warning was in force. There was little traffic, as the majority of the vehicles, including the buses, were at the front. The streets and squares were lined with huge banks of snow. The restaurants and shops were open, but dancing was forbidden. Many homes in the city had a call from the local priest to announce the death of a husband, father, brother or son in action at the front. Since the dead were normally returned to their home districts, a beautiful area in the Hietaniemi Cemetery was set aside for their burial. This became the resting place of about 1700 soldiers from Helsinki who fell in the Winter War.

The Interim Peace of 1940–1941

The Foreign Minister Väinö Tanner announced the end of the war on 13th March 1940 and explained the arduous conditions attached to it. The army was gradually demobilized and the many military authorities and central administrative bodies returned to Helsinki. The brief period of peace that followed the Winter War – referred to later as the Interim Peace – was overshadowed throughout by an awareness of the consequences of the Great War being waged in Europe. The aggression shown by the major powers had led to the demise of many of the smaller nations. The June 1940 the Soviet Union occupied Estonia, Latvia and Lithuania, and by the time Germany had occupied Norway and Denmark, it was difficult for Finland to import foodstuffs from anywhere other than Germany.

The dangers that the country had been through during the Winter War had created a strong sense of comradeship. Finland had been united in its struggle, since all sectors of society perceived the Soviet Union as an aggressor, and defence of the fatherland was a matter of common concern. Immediately after the war, servicemen's organizations sprang up to support the families and relatives of those who had been killed or wounded. There were just a few people, mostly communist leaders who had been in protective detention during the war, who set up a "Society for peace and friendship between Finland and the Soviet Union" in Helsinki. The demonstrations held by this group regularly led to confrontations with the representatives of law and order, as such activities were generally regarded as aimed at destroying the inner strength that the Finnish nation had developed.

Under the new division of Finland into military provinces (including Civil Guard districts) that came into force in 1940, following the Winter War, Helsinki formed a province of its own, with 33 569 men registered as capable of bearing arms. About half of these consisted of infantrymen, light troops and men belonging to the higher ranks of the General Staff. These officers and specialized men were sent to other military provinces that had a shortage of them. Rearmament continued, and by the winter of 1941 sufficient field weapons and equipment were in store in the places from which the troops were to be gathered. Thus the weapons needed by the men from Helsinki were ready for them there and not somewhere on the border.

Tension between Germany and the Soviet Union was growing all the time, and the situation in Europe was such by the early summer of 1941 that Finland ordered a general mobilization of troops once more. This took place on 17th June. The men of Helsinki were once again fitted out for service in the border regions. The 12th Division, or Helsinki Division, commanded by Colonel E.A. Vihma, was transported mostly by road to South-Eastern Finland and stations in the Miehikkälä area.

The Continuation War of 1941–1945

Operation Barbarossa, the great German offensive against the Soviet Union, began on 22nd June 1941. The Finnish government announced that it would remain neutral but would defend itself if attacked by the Soviet Union. Neutrality lasted just three days. The air raid sirens in Helsinki sounded again at 8.50 a.m. on 25th June, and the Prime Minister, speaking to Parliament, indicated that he considered Finland to be once more at war with the Soviet Union. The army headquarters was moved back to Mikkeli, but both Parliament and the cabinet decided to remain in Helsinki. President Ryti moved to a new villa at Tamminiemi, close to the island of Seurasaari, which had been donated for the use of the Head of State.

Helsinki was again seriously threatened from the air, and now the Soviet forces had the whole of Estonia available from which to mount their attacks. But the Finnish defence forces were stronger than at the time of the Winter War. The Air Force succeeded in shooting down a number of enemy bombers, which now attacked by night as well as in the daytime, and Helsinki was protected by seven navy anti-aircraft batteries, four light divisions, two anti-aircraft rifle platoons and six

The city's efficient air defences, which were partly reliant on German radar equipment, functioned particularly successfully during the Continuation War of 1941–44.

searchlight platoons. Later, in 1943, efficient new anti-aircraft defence equipment was obtained from Germany.

The rapid advance of the Germans on the eastern front attracted the main attention of the Russians at first and Helsinki was mostly left in peace. A few reconnaissance flights were made, and one or two bombs were dropped on the city in connection with these. The situation then improved markedly when the Germans occupied Estonia, so that the Russians lost the use of their bases there. At the same time, in September 1941, Finland succeeded in recapturing the ceded areas on the Karelian Isthmus, and this was followed in the course of the autumn by the conquest of Eastern Karelia.

The people of Helsinki did not escape to the safety of the country-side to the same extent as during the Winter War, partly because the city now had more air-raid shelters. Again it was necessary to employ wartime lighting, i.e. the windows of the houses were covered during the hours of darkness and the street lights were turned down to a blue glow. As the war dragged on it was also necessary to begin air-raid patrols, to prevent criminal elements from breaking into homes and shops. All men aged 16–60 years still present in the city, of whom there were about 30 000, were obliged to take turns in this, forming two-man patrols. The system proved efficient and remained in force until the end of the war.

With the majority of the male population capable of working away from home, many families found it difficult to make ends meet. The obligatory labour laws required everyone to make their contribution to keeping the wheels turning in the countryside and in the towns, and many people in Helsinki were engaged in voluntary work. Gas was in short supply in Helsinki and had to be rationed, and there were some logs to be had, but there was not enough coal for any to be released for general consumption. The vehicles ran on producer gas. All foodstuffs were difficult to come by in the winter of 1941−1942, but the shortages were relieved somewhat in the subsequent war years by supplies received from Germany. The main entertainments were the request concerts arranged by the Propaganda Comrades and the wide range of programmes provided at the army concert parties. Contacts with the front were obtained through the great exhibitions of material captured in battle and of handicrafts made by different divisions of the troops in off-duty moments.

When the tide began to turn against Germany in February 1943, Finland was ready to disengage from the war, but this process was complicated by the complex bonds which the country had with Germany by that time. At their conference in Teheran at the New Year 1944, the Soviet Union and the Western powers declared one of their targets to be to take the countries fighting alongside Germany out of the war. This included Finland. The Soviet Union began to increase the pressure with large-scale bombing raids on Helsinki. In the first phase of this assault, on 6th February, 130 Russian planes in formations of 1−8 at a time targeted in on the capital, but the anti-aircraft defences worked at full stretch, and evidently for this reason the Soviet assailants dropped their bombs well before the city itself and turned tail. The following day they were more successful. In the course of the two

The intensified Soviet bombing in February 1944 increased the pressure on the city. Although relatively few bombs actually fell on it, one of them penetrated to "the heart of the nation", hitting the main building of the university. This was regarded as a severe loss. In the centre of the picture is the statue to Emperor Alexander II, unveiled in 1894.

days about 1500 bombs were dropped in the areas outside Helsinki, 58 in the suburbs and 248 high-explosive bombs and 25 incendiary bombs on the city itself. Almost 250 brick, stone and wooden buildings were damaged or destroyed, 88 people were killed and several hundred were injured. About 102 000 people were evacuated from Helsinki when the bombing started.

Meanwhile the Finnish leadership had begun to explore the possibility of opening negotiations with Moscow. The Helsinki air defences had been strengthened after the first assault, and the Soviet Union had then stepped up its attacks, employing its long-range forces under Air Marshal Golovanov. On 16th February 1941 the anti-aircraft battery again received warning in good time and succeeded in preventing a major bombing of the city. The third large-scale attack came ten days later, at the same time as the Finnish negotiator, J.K. Paasikivi arrived home from Stockholm, bringing the Soviet Union's preliminary conditions for peace with him.

In the last, most powerful and most exhausting air raid of all, on 26th February, Helsinki was bombed in three phases. The first evening attack failed, and again showed the effectiveness of the air defences, the decisive element in which was the radar equipment obtained from Germany. The majority of the bombs fell in the sea, but the few which hit the city started 15 fires. The most dramatic atmosphere was caused by the main building of the University catching fire. The second wave, before and after midnight, was repelled still more efficient-

Helsinki suffered from numerous Soviet bombing raids during the Second World War. As soon as a raid began the people had to make for the air raid shelters.

ly, and only a small fraction of the 150 or so aircraft managed to drop their bombs on the city. The third phase then began in the early hours of the morning, when about 200 planes attacked from different directions, but again relatively few bombs fell on the actual city itself. The damage to buildings was worst in the southern and central parts, and altogether some 1500 people were left homeless.

The large-scale bombing raids on Helsinki in February 1944 were thus repelled with very few losses. The results were quite unique for the whole of the Second World War. About 1500 bomber flights were made over the city, and the number of bombs dropped was about ten times this figure, but only 799 of these, just over 5%, landed in the city area. Altogether 109 buildings were destroyed and 150 lives were lost, not even one in a thousand of the population. The Soviet members of the Control Commission set up in the city on the cessation of hostilities were amazed that there was scarcely any damage to be seen. One thing that made the task of the anti-aircraft detachments easier was that the enemy planes flew in from the east or south-east in a continuous stream. If the long-range forces had operated in the "English style" and concentrated hundreds of planes above the city for an hour or two, arriving from different directions and at different altitudes, it would have been impossible to eliminate them all. This was what was done over the German cities.

After the events of February the enemy apparently lost interest in bombing Helsinki, although preparations had been made for occupying the city. Instead, the Russians concentrated their major offensives in summer 1944 on the Karelian Isthmus, although still without being able to achieve any final breakthrough. It was at that point that the Commander-in-Chief, Mannerheim, was elected President under an emergency Act of Parliament and began to guide the country towards peace. Relations with Germany were broken off and hostilities directed against the Soviet Union came to an end in September 1944.

Elsewhere in the world it was the normal practice to bury the dead in mass graves on the field of battle, but the Finns made every effort to return the fallen for burial in the soil of their home districts. Thus the majority of the men from Helsinki who were killed in the war are buried in the Hietaniemi Cemetery, along with a number of German soldiers. In 1951, Marshal Mannerheim himself was laid to rest among the war heroes whom he had commanded, and it has been customary ever since that time for thousands of students to visit the war graves at Hietaniemi on Independence Day, 6th December, each year and to march in a torchbearing procession from there to the Senate Square,

performing what is symbolically one of the most important acts of re-
membrance by the Finnish people.

The collapse of the Berlin Wall altered the Finns' attitudes towards
their memories of the war. At last they could speak more freely of
their wartime experiences. Marshal Mannerheim and President Risto
Ryti, who had been the central figures in the Continuation War, were
voted the "greatest of the Finns" in a television ballot, and large numbers of accounts of the war in the form of research reports, books and
plays have been written. Also, many details of the darker sides of the
war, such as the Finnish prisoner-of-war camps, have emerged alongside the tales of heroism. The national defence and war veterans' associations have gained new active members in recent times, and the
numbers of people joining voluntary defence organizations have increased. Many men and women, young and old, have formed security
and civil guard companies and many reservists have joined the newly
created provincial troops, to be trained by the Defence Forces in cooperation with other related organizations and the police and rescue
services.

(This chapter is based on the article "Helsinki in the Second World
War, 1939–1945" written in Finnish by T. V. Viljanen for Vol. V of the
History of the City of Helsinki" (1964).

The people of
Helsinki gathered in
the Station Square
to celebrate the end
of the Second World
War in Finland.

HELSINKI GROWS INTO A METROPOLIS

"We have to resign ourselves to the fact that the population centres, and particularly the large cities, will draw people to them like magnets in the future. Fortunately there are people who don't care for the peace of a detached house or the closeness to nature of a garden city but, in spite of sociologists' opinions to the contrary, actually want to live in the midst of the busiest form of life possible."

(Teuvo Aura, Chairman of Helsinki City Council, 1965)

How did Helsinki manage with modernizing its urban structure and traffic, the same task that faced all the larger European cities during the period of post-war reconstruction? Urban growth around Helsinki before the war had been concentrated mainly beside the main railway lines and along the coast in both directions. The population of the capital in 1944 had been about 275 000. The new age of greater mobility could already be seen in the main roads built during the 1930's, Porvoontie and Jorvaksentie, but otherwise the area beyond the city boundary was still traditionally agrarian in character in immediate post-war times, with all the landscape elements and ways of life that went with this.

The idea had already been raised in the Ministry of the Interior in the 1920's that the suburban areas that lay beyond the city boundaries could be incorporated into the city. It was regarded as important that the area dominated economically by Helsinki, which in any case comprised only about 30 km², should be placed under one local government authority and one system of urban planning, so that more efficient use could be made of its building land. The background to this was the real situation as it was in the suburbs, for earlier surveys had suggested that living and dwelling standards in self-governing suburban areas were on average lower than those that ought to belong to an urban environment. The question of incorporation gave rise to much argument for and against. Some of the suburbs were in favour of joining the capital, while others, the more prosperous and self-sufficient ones, were against it.

Eventually the war years made it essential to join forces and extend the boundaries of Helsinki, as the rapid growth in population in the district as a whole increased the pressures to achieve an overall solution to the problem. Under the first legislation to this effect, passed in October 1944, the rural districts of Huopalahti, Oulunkylä and Kulosaari, the borough of Haaga and the communities of Lauttasaari,

Munkkiniemi, Pakinkylä (later known as Pakila) and Degerö (Laajasalo), together with Viikki, Vartiokylä, Malmi, Tapanila, Pukinmäki and Puistola and a few other small areas, were all incorporated within Helsinki from the beginning of 1946. This gave the capital some 51 000 new inhabitants and multiplied its area by a factor of five, to 163 km² The later annexation of Vuosaari in 1966 increased this figure by another 15 km² to the level at which it stands today.

The war as such left the city with relatively few signs of damage, but the restoration of peace led to a busy spate of building which continued with only minor interruptions until the early 1970's. The first stage, repair of the buildings that had been destroyed or damaged in the bombing, was relatively soon completed, and the main building of the University, restored almost entirely to its original form, was reopened in 1948, but the second and far more demanding phase was the provision of housing for the increasing flood of new population into the city.

Helsinki was developing into a metropolis at a rapid pace and on all fronts at once. By the early 1950's the administrators were speaking of the needs occasioned by this "dynamic community development". The organization of traffic and transport, the provision of an infrastructure, planning and building in the suburban areas and redesigning of the city centre headed the list of priorities. More and more offices were being built in the centre, and the residential areas round the periphery began to expand, so that commuting from the subur-

Dwellings for the industrial employees of Kone ja Silta Oy, designed by the architects Armas Lindgren and Bertel Liljeqvist, were built in the Vallila area in the 1910's and 1920's. This block is an excellent example of social dwelling house construction in the post-World War I period in terms of its architecture and the uniformity of appearance that it bestowed on the area.

Attempts were made to channel the post-war flow of migration towards the new suburban areas of the city. This is a general view of Northern Haaga, built in the late 1950's. The forests and closeness to nature were an essential part of suburban living at that time.

ban areas became more common. This trend obviously met with approval, as everything possible was done to promote the conversion of old residential blocks near the centre into offices.

The greatest problem with which the capital has had to wrestle since the war has been a shortage of dwellings. In September 1945 the Helsinki bureau for rented accommodation had 5800 applications for places to live, mostly from families with children, but only a few hundred dwellings to offer. Families, students, men returning from the war and war invalids were accommodated for a long time in prefabricated buildings and temporary premises such as air-raid shelters, night lodgings, hostels, hotels and sub-let rooms in dwellings where every room, including the kitchen, had to be occupied on account of the rationing regulations. The shortage of homes led to cramped living conditions, dissatisfaction and all kinds of speculation. There was a shortage of water and of firewood, and hot water was also rationed. The question was raised at one time as to whether people should be forbidden from moving to the city, and a permit system was tried out for a few years. Students without accommodation held numerous demonstrations as a means of appealing to the owners of dwellings in Helsinki.

The increase in population was faster in the newly incorporated areas than in the city proper, and it was there that the greatest pressure for new building existed. It had still been the case even in the 1940's that more building had taken place in the city centre than in the suburbs, but by the next decade the construction of new dwelling houses was clearly focused on the outlying areas. Some temporary wooden buildings were put up in previously uninhabited forested areas immediately after the war, but this manner of building, which can scarcely be said to have been urban in character, came to an end in 1947, mainly on account of the generally difficult economic situation. In practice, however, some of those dwellings were still being used until the early 1970's.

Helsinki was by no means exceptional as far as the post-war housing situation was concerned, however, for conditions were equally catastrophic in many other parts of the country for a long time. The government had no clear housing policy, nor was there any national body that was formally responsible for such matters. The crucial step as far as initiating local authority house building was concerned was the "Arava" legislation of 1949, under which low-interest state loans were made available for the building of dwellings intended for private ownership. This provided a key to the Helsinki housing problem, too, the first building financed under this scheme taking place at Ruskeasuo and Maunula.

The building of apartment blocks spread outside the city centre in the 1950's on account of the more frequent possession of motor cars, which made longer journeys to work and to shops, offices, etc. feasible. Thus the focus in the provision of new housing shifted from estates of small, mainly detached houses to areas of apartment blocks. The first extensive areas of this kind after Maunula grew up at Herttoniemi, Roihuvuori, Lauttasaari, Munkkivuori, Haaga and Munkkiniemi, the accent during the following decade being on Pihlajamäki, Jakomäki, Kontula, Laajasalo, Myllypuro and Puotila. By the end of the 1960's the focal point of this building activity had already moved beyond the boundaries of Helsinki into the areas of the neighbouring local authorities, giving rising to the suburbs of Myyrmäki, Martinlaakso, Tikkurila, Pähkinärinne, Olari, Suvela and others.

Almost without exception it was the areas of land acquired by the individual contractors that determined the direction in which new building advanced and the extent of this building. The continuous purchase of land was essential to the existence of any building company, as there was no land to be had which had already been planned for building. Thus there gradually emerged a pattern of building typical of the Greater Helsinki region in which a whole area was developed at once, the aim being to achieve a more efficient, mass production style of building. The first whole suburb to be constructed in this way was Pihlajamäki, and the model of financing the purchase of such apartments through saving accounts opened for this purpose begun there was later applied to other areas. This construction of whole residential areas at one time was also economical as far as the local authorities were concerned. All that was needed was to draw up district plans for the land acquired by the building company for a given minimum permitted building volume, and the building companies themselves would attend to the infrastructure. The reaction of the general public to this activity may perhaps be summed up best by the somewhat pejorative connotations attached to the new word for "property developer" which it introduced into the Finnish language. There was a definite feeling that a kind of "old boys' network" existed between the heads of the building companies, the banks and the local planning authorities. Private individuals' savings accounts were harnessed to serve the interests of the rapid mechanization of building techniques and the concluding of large contracts covering whole residential areas at a time.

It was during the post-war reconstruction period that the model community for urban development in the Helsinki region emerged: the forest suburb. The pattern of land ownership (in which there was an abundance of building land available), the development of new construction techniques and the line taken by the local authorities all favoured the building of a new suburb directly in the forest. The custom of distributing settlement in isolated cells combined with the "neighbourhood principle" became established as the only conceivable point of departure in town planning. New suburbs were no

The scourges of big cities, private cars and traffic jams, began to make themselves felt in Helsinki in the 1960's.

longer joined on to the existing urban structures but were located so as to be surrounded entirely by an area of land left in its natural state. The authority on this philosophy of planning was Otto-Iivari Meurman, Professor of Town Planning at the Helsinki University of Technology, who had set out the framework for this in his textbook published in 1947, where he justified it in terms of the aim to fashion the suburban apartment block into a suitable model for family accommodation.

The Helsinki style of suburban building reflects the ideological and political priorities of the post-war reconstruction period. It was essential to ensure the survival of democracy and the future of the family. Efforts were made to avoid post-war crises by strengthening people's sense of community, dispelling loneliness and improving living conditions for families with children. More than 50% of the population were still employed in agriculture and forestry, and the accent within national housing policy was on guaranteeing the economic viability of the countryside and resettling the refugees from the ceded territories and the servicemen returning from the front. The war had left 420 000 people homeless, 11% of the total population, and since there were not enough jobs in industry to provide a living for them, more small farms were created in the countryside. This policy also found support in the ideological abhorrence of towns that still prevailed at that time, whereby it was believed that the "problem of flight from the countryside" could be resolved by founding new rural

Puotinharju represents the typical Helsinki suburban architecture of the 1960's. It grew up to the east of the city centre, which was the main direction of expansion at that time. This view of the shopping centre shows that these "cities in the forest" were dormitory suburbs dominated by blocks of flats.

communities. These measures simply delayed the restructuring of the nation by about twenty years.

The "forest suburb" was a convenient combination of a natural and an urban environment. Nature emerged once more as a condition for a good, harmonious life, even in the town, as an antidote to rented "barracks" accommodation. In fact, Helsinki had already been an overcrowded city even in the 1930's, as the average residential block in the centre in 1938 had 88 inhabitants, whereas the corresponding figure for Berlin was 76 and that for Paris 38.

The best-known area of new building close to Helsinki in the 1950's was the garden city of Tapiola, which rose to the status of a national symbol. It was built under the auspices of a private social organization and immediately on the edge of the Helsinki area, only eight kilometres from the city centre. The accent throughout was on nature, individuality and the importance of the family. The home and the natural environment emerged to create harmony out of the harsh world of rational labour and efficient production. Tapiola was designed for the use of the ideal human type of the post-war reconstruction period – the family-centred, outdoor person – and the result was a model suburb which held a particular attraction for the educated middle class. Indeed, it soon came to be known as "the better folks' village".

Helsinki has changed greatly during post-war times, both internally and geographically. The new suburbs of the 1950's and 1960's attracted large numbers of families with children, both from the overcrowded accommodation of the city centre and directly from the countryside. Many of these people were attracted by the more spacious way of living, which they longed for eagerly, together with the high standards of amenities and the closeness to nature. The Helsinki style of urbanism came into being most naturally in the suburbs, on the boundary between town and country. One consequence was that the population of the city proper, both the centre and the residential areas to the south of it, decreased steadily until the early 1990's, so that where it had had some 260 000 inhabitants in 1962, the figure had dropped to only about 160 000 by 1987. By contrast, the suburban population grew from 195 000 to almost 325 000 over the same period, the highest rates of growth being in the eastern and north-eastern parts of the metropolitan area.

The most intensive phase of urban building occurred in the 1970's and 1980's, when it was undoubtedly felt that more had to be built, more efficiently and more densely if the target of 600 000 inhabitants laid down by the city administrators was to be achieved. The first

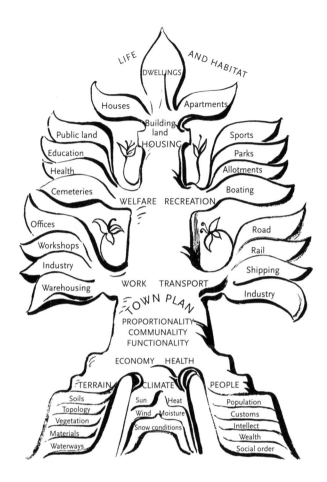

LIFE AND HABITAT
DWELLINGS
Houses / Apartments
Building land
Public land
HOUSING
Education
Health
Sports
Cemeteries
Parks
WELFARE RECREATION
Allotments
Boating
Offices
Road
Workshops
Rail
Industry
Shipping
Warehousing
WORK TRANSPORT
Industry
TOWN PLAN
PROPORTIONALITY
COMMUNALITY
FUNCTIONALITY
ECONOMY HEALTH
TERRAIN CLIMATE PEOPLE
Soils
Sun Heat
Population
Topology
Wind Moisture
Customs
Vegetation
Snow conditions
Intellect
Materials
Wealth
Waterways
Social order

Otto-I. Meurman, who had worked in the office headed by the architect Eliel Saarinen, became the first professor of town planning in Finland. His urban ideal was a situation in which nature predominated over the achievements of man, and he used to depict the essence of his ideas in the form of a tree diagram. Meurman did much to introduce contemporary international notions of town planning into Finland.

areas to be used for new building were those adjacent to existing suburbs, before the changeover in the 1970's to large-scale development projects covering whole areas at once, whereupon the favourite locations tended to be alongside the fastest railway lines. This led to a dense urban structure in the Malmi-Tapanila-Pukinmäki-Puistola area, in Haaga, Kannelmäki and Malminkartano and in the eastern suburbs along the route of the metro, especially in Vuosaari. The other main urban centres to be created in addition to Tapiola were Malmi and Itäkeskus (the East City).

Life in the suburbs has added new elements to the Helsinki urban identity. People's relationship with nature has become important

Tapiola Garden City, built right on the border of Helsinki proper, was internationally the best-known and most respected of the products of Finnish post-war urban planning.

when buying a home and when choosing how to spend their leisure time. Community values are maintained by the non-political residents' associations and suburban organizations, which take it upon themselves to bring matters of importance to their area before the local government bodies concerned and keep an eye on the progress of planning and building. Large numbers of these residents' associations were formed in the golden years of suburban building in the 1950's and 1960's, and they did much to inspire a community spirit, to shape urban traditions (celebrations, anniversaries, voluntary work etc.) and to record people's recollections and memories. Sport and outdoor recreation plays a large part in maintaining and communicating a local spirit, and this has been especially true of ice hockey, where the modern, commercially managed Helsinki team "Jokerit" has had

The golden years of suburban expansion were in the 1960's, when large housing areas were built at a rapid rate with the aim of attracting mainly families with children. These apartments were light, modern and well appointed.

116

a considerable effect in creating a sense of identity on the east side of the city in particular.

Development in the Helsinki area was at its height during the formative period for the major cities in Finland in the 1960's, and it was in 1965 that the city's population reached half a million. By this stage, in fact, population growth was extending rapidly towards the edges of the city's administrative area, progressively further from the centre, and the functions that had previously been associated with the city centre were now being dispersed into a regional network. Where the majority of the population growth in the region in the 1950's and 1960's was concentrated in the city of Helsinki itself, it tended in subsequent years to focus increasingly on the surrounding local authorities, first of all mainly the borough of Espoo (which became the town in 1972) and the rural district of Helsinki (which became the borough of Vantaa in 1972 and a town in 1974). In this way the concept of Greater Helsinki was born, referring to the four local authorities in the metropolitan area, those mentioned above together with Kauniainen (which became a borough in 1920 and a town in 1972). Before very long, however, the same term began to be applied to a much wider area that included surrounding districts such as Kirkkonummi, Kerava, Hyvinkää, Riihimäki, Järvenpää, Tuusula and Sipoo.

Cooperation between the local authorities in and around Helsinki has been politically a constantly recurring theme over the last 40 years or so, and one that has also been of interest to the central government. The aim initially was a form of voluntary consultation in matters of district planning, coordination of public transport, the creation of infrastructure networks (water supplies, sewerage and waste disposal) and the amalgamation of hospital services. The Ministry of the Interior was in favour of a great merger of local authorities in the 1960's which would have turned Helsinki, Espoo, Kauniainen and the Helsinki rural district into one gigantic administrative unit, but their plan met with severe opposition as the districts were reluctant to abandon their actively functioning independent authorities and substantial differences of opinion about the advantages of a large organization. The authorities themselves preferred to keep control over forms of cooperation in their own hands. One problem lay in the administrative differences between the city of Helsinki and the surrounding boroughs and rural districts and the special nature of each when it came to matters of planning and building in particular, although the same was also true in the spheres of culture, social welfare and health. Helsinki possessed an urban council structure with a large body of administra-

The old wooden buildings in the centre of Helsinki were threatened with demolition in the 1950's and 1960's. The picture shows the Skoha building opposite the Central Railway Station which was demolished in 1966–67 to make way for the complex of shops and offices that came to be known as "Makkaratalo", the Sausage House. Both epitomize the contemporary architecture of their day.

"The new, elegant Aikatalo" in Mikonkatu behind the Atheneum represents the modernist view of the reform of urban structure in the 1950's.

tors, whereas local government in the rural districts was carried on in quite a different spirit. The eventual solution was the Helsinki Metropolitan Area Council, which was assigned the task of coordinating cooperation between the authorities, preparing proposals for regional cooperation and representing the whole region in dealings with the central government.

Although the Metropolitan Area Council has now been functioning for 30 years, it has not by any means been able to carry out all the joint projects on the list drafted by the local authorities in 1970. Some of them have been transferred to other organizations created for the purpose, such as the provision of recreation areas and the acquisition of water for domestic supplies, and some have eventually been implemented by the various councils separately. Also, in view of the continued migration of population into the Helsinki region, increasing deliberations have been held in the 1980's and 1990's over how to include the fringe districts in this cooperation model as well, especially now that there are eight such local authorities whose population is growing faster than that of either Helsinki or Vantaa, namely Hyvinkää, Järvenpää, Kerava, Kirkkonummi, Nurmijärvi, Tuusula, Sipoo and Vihti. Their power of attraction is increasing at the same time as that of Helsinki itself is diminishing on account of the shortage of housing and building plots. The peripheral districts can meet the demand for private houses and terraced houses better than can any other authorities in the metropolitan region. At the same time the present level of growth provides an opportunity for filling in the somewhat dispersed community structure of the region and for improving the standards of services.

Major changes were made to the centre of Helsinki in the postwar period, especially when the sale of permits for additional building on existing plots in the late 1950's or early 1960's increased the pressure for new building and the demolition of old houses. One consequence was that a dozen or so beautiful old stone buildings in the Neo-Renaissance style and numerous old commercial buildings were destroyed to make way for modern constructions. The southern end of Helsinki's main thoroughfare, Mannerheimintie, and the area around the railway station were "modernized" to the extent that they became practically unrecognizable within a few years. A number of new buildings in the latest continental style were created for the people of that time to admire, including the Olympic Pavilion, the Elanto department store on Aleksanterinkatu, the Palace, Vaakuna and Marski Hotels, and the Aikatalo and Kaivotalo pedestrian precincts. Examples of modern office architecture include the Autotalo building in the

Kamppi area, the head offices of the Enso-Gutzeit Company overlooking the Market Place, the Makkaratalo ("Sausage House") complex on the corner of Kaivokatu and Keskuskatu, the City Council offices in the Kallio district, the circular shopping precinct Ympyrätalo and the Akateeminen Kirjakauppa building on the North Esplanade.

Other rebuilding operations that took place around the same time involved the demolition of old wooden buildings from the Empire period and their replacement with stone and element-built ones. Whole areas of the city that were remodelled in this way included Kallio, Sörnäinen, Alppiharju, Punavuori and Ullanlinna. The people of Helsinki began to object to this policy only in the late 1960's, when the threat to demolish the old Hotel Kämp and the new area plans for the streets of wooden houses in Vallila and for the Käpylä area gave rise to a popular movement demanding their preservation. The attitudes of the development companies began to change. The Hotel Kämp was replaced with a replica and the Vallila and Käpylä areas were allowed to keep their original plans. Similarly, some of the old villas in the Ruoholahti district were retained. Since that time repeated battles have been fought for the preservation of old buildings, although actual wooden houses are scarce now that the western part of Pasila has been rebuilt. One or two 19th century wooden buildings from elsewhere in the city have now been moved to the shore at Kaisaniemi to remind passers-by of the scale of building as it was in the Helsinki of the Empire period.

One inescapable element in "dynamic urban development" is an increase in traffic volumes. The stream of goods and vehicles coming into Helsinki from the surrounding areas has required major investments in road construction. A decision was made in the 1950's, in fact, in view of the unemployment situation, to improve or rebuild all the main roads radiating out of the capital. It was around that time that the city was seized by a motor mania on the pattern of that already experienced in the outside world, when it was believed that it was every person's right to own a car. The trunk road to Pori was opened during the same decade, and the first properly surfaced "autostrada" of international proportions, the motorway leading out of the city in the direction of Turku, was inaugurated in 1960. The main urban freeways were built shortly afterwards, that to the east being completed in 1962 and that to the west four years later. The brand-new motorway north to Tuusula was functioning by 1968, and work on renewing the road to Lahti was eventually finished in 1973. These roads have been widened and improved in many places in more recent times, and a direct four-lane motorway from Helsinki to Tampere was opened in the early 1990's. The conversion of the entire length of the road from Helsinki to Lahti into a motorway on the strength of private funding was completed by the beginning of the new millennium.

The most extensive post-war building project of all in Helsinki itself was the development of the suburban rail network. Plans for an express network had been in existence since the beginning of the century, and work was begun after the war on re-designing this system in order to link the various parts of the city by a network of railway and tram lines. The idea of a separate underground line had been raised in the late 1940's, when the Suburban Transport Committee was set up to plan public transport routes for the whole city area. The proposed line soon came to be referred to as the Metro, after the world-famous systems in Paris and St. Petersburg, and eventually a separate Metro Committee was appointed in 1959. Four years later it submitted its proposals for a system of fast electric trains operating below ground in the city centre.

The people of Helsinki had been keeping a careful eye on devel-

A new mode of transport, the Metro, became available for the first time in 1982. This "express tramway" that ran partly underground had been planned for several decades.

opments elsewhere during the 1950's, particularly the building of underground lines in Stockholm and Toronto, but even after the City Council had approved the report of the Metro Committee in 1965 there were numerous political, logistic and financial differences of opinion to be resolved before work could begin. Public doubts regarding the whole scheme increased towards the late 1960's, especially on the grounds of expense. Meanwhile the American consultants Wilbur Smith and Associates, together with the Finnish firm of Pentti Polvinen, had come up with a grandiose scheme which advocated support for private motoring and the building of massive arterial roads in the city. This proposal aroused much lively public discussion, and the outcome was exactly the opposite, a decision to favour public transport.

The joint deliberations of the Finnish Railways and the Helsinki City Council on a basic rail network to serve the northern, northwestern and western sectors of the metropolitan area gained new impetus in the 1970's. A decision had been made that the new residential areas in Helsinki, Espoo and Vantaa should be located beside electrified lines, and electrification of the suburban lines around Helsinki was completed in 1969–1972. In addition, a new line to Martinlaakso was inaugurated in 1975. Work on developing the rail system continued into the 1990's with an agreement to build an urban line to Tikkurila. Development of a second, "metro-type" urban line between Helsinki and Leppävaara began in the late 1990's.

The final decision on the route for the Metro was taken in 1971, allowing for the construction of a basic underground line from Hakaniemi via the main railway station to Kamppi. The building of the whole line from Kamppi to the East City terminal lasted virtually the whole decade, and the first bright red Metro train set out from Hakaniemi to the East City on 1st June 1982. The line was extended to Kamppi a year later, further east to Kontula in 1986 and on to Mellunmäki three years later. The line to Vuosaari was opened in 1998. In time the line was continued westwards to Ruoholahti, and the Kaisaniemi station in the centre was opened to the public in 1993. A decision in principle was taken in Espoo in 1998 to support the continuation of the Metro westwards to Tapiola, and this was followed in 2006 by a decision to extend the plans to cover the whole Espoo area. The actual construction work is due to start some time after 2010 at the earliest. The Metro is an expensive system, but it has become an essential part of the city's transport network and carries more than 140 000 passengers a day speedily and efficiently.

The planning and building of the Metro has been accompanied at every turn by an avid public debate on the need for such a project, and particularly on its cost. The City Council has been accused of megalomania and of over-ambitious planning, and its public image was tarnished somewhat in the 1980's by a long court case in which certain high-up council officials were accused of accepting bribes in connection with the building of the Metro. At the same time it must be said that the Metro has not threatened in any way the existence of the tram system, which is an integral part of the spirit of the city. Although many of the large European cities have dispensed with their trams in their enthusiasm to build underground railways, Helsinki set about developing its tram system further in the 1950's and acquiring up-to-date vehicles. The greatest controversy on this front was the trial of strength between the City Transport Department and the citizens' organizations over retaining the traditional green and yellow colours of the trams in the 1980's.

As in many other large cities in Europe, the fragmentation of the urban structure, the degeneration of the city centre and the unrestricted growth of private motor traffic has given rise to general concern for the future. "The city and its people have become too mechanical" claimed one pamphlet produced in Helsinki in 1974. Urban building, with its emphasis on economic efficiency and technical devices filled ordinary citizens, researchers, architects and town planners with anxiety over the potential destruction of the social and cultural life of the urban community. People began to speak of "urban erosion" caused by the growth in traffic and of the possible consequences of this. The city of the motor car and the metro was seen as a place which was becoming increasingly difficult to live in and where the environment was deteriorating all the time. "There is less and less space for people", the architects Mikael Sundman and Vilhelm Helander wrote in their highly controversial pamphlet *Whose Helsinki?* in 1970.

It was only in the 1970's that attitudes changed and respect for the city was restored, when people elsewhere in the world began to appreciate better the importance of downtown areas as arenas for lively social interaction. The need for such a change of heart was all the more apparent in Helsinki because the concentration of jobs in the centre was causing a huge increase in traffic. A pedestrians' and cyclists' association "Majority", founded in 1968, was particularly active in drawing attention to the pollution and noise caused by private cars in the centre and in arguing for a change in traffic policy on the part of the City Council in favour of public transport. They received considerable support from the public at large in these matters and serious efforts were indeed made in the 1970's to improve public transport. One further factor instrumental in bringing about the change in attitudes was the debate over rail and metro transport referred to above.

The town plan for the central area adopted in the 1970's also represented a change in attitude. Unrestricted development was no longer looked on kindly, and positive steps were taken to limit the widespread conversion of city centre properties into offices, to improve the environment in which people lived and to maintain standards of services. The first ideas on inner city regeneration also spread to Finland around that time, and a decision was taken as early as 1969 to experiment with taking the traffic away from Aleksanterinkatu entirely. Another busy street, Iso-Roobertinkatu, was converted to a pedestrian way in the European style in the 1970's, although the measure has not been particularly successful. The street does not join up with any other pedestrian precincts and it has not proved possible to restrict motor traffic to a sufficient degree. In general, the cramped traffic conditions on the peninsula of central Helsinki mean that it is virtually impossible to create an uninterrupted network of pedestrian streets.

Many local traders' associations, such as Espa, representing the shops in the Esplanade area, have tried to stimulate the smaller shops and boutiques and create more atmosphere in the city. An opportunity arose to refurbish the valuable old buildings around the Senate Square in the 1980's, when the police and city court that had been housed in them were moved to new premises in Pasila, and the fortifications of Suomenlinna (Sveaborg) were returned to their former glory in time for their 250th anniversary in 1998. Major projects for improving the Kaivopuisto and Esplanade parks have been carried out in recent years, Mikonkatu has been restricted to pedestrians only, the North Esplanade has been widened and the functionalist-style Glass Palace has been restored as a multi-purpose building. The city's network of cycle tracks has been extended and made more useful, and the old bus station building has been renovated with loving care.

The city centre was rescued from many of the pressures of renovation and new building by the choice of Pasila as an alternative area for many of its functions. A total of some 35 000 jobs and 20 000 homes were moved there, making it a major development undertaking even by international standards. The eastern part of the area was developed in the 1970's to form a very dense concentration of offices, services and businesses, with some residential buildings as well. A new exhibition hall and main library were also built there. A great deal of criticism was levelled at the whole area at the time, however, on account

of the height of the buildings, their ponderous scale, the confused pedestrian arrangements and the poor architectural standards of the largely element-built blocks. When the western area was designed some time later to be mostly residential in character, the buildings were made lower and more varied in appearance and followed the contours of the terrain and the old network of streets. Another extensive residential area built close to the centre in the 1970's is Merihaka, located in a landfill area extended out into the sea. The main focal points for such building in more recent decades have been the tip of Katajanokka and Ruoholahti.

The age distribution of the population in the city centre has been turned upside down over the last twenty years. In the 1970's it was still mainly elderly people who lived in the centre, while the young people and families preferred the suburbs and outlying areas. The intensive migration towards the Helsinki region that has taken place in the 1990's has brought a new wave of residents to the city centre, however, at the same time as the people who established themselves in the suburbs after the war are gradually approaching retiring age and their children have moved away to start families of their own in the newer areas on the metropolitan fringe. Rents and selling prices of single-room apartments in the city centre rose sharply in the economic boom years of the 1980's and again in the late 1990's, after the recession had subsided.

Innovations such the Motor Building, the Tennis Hall and the Kamppi Market Place give expression to the metropolitan ideals of the 20th century. This photograph from 1962 shows the emergence of a central business district at the heart of Helsinki, close to the Bus Station, introducing people to international trends in urban architecture.

The people moving to Helsinki have throughout the years represented the younger end of the age range, men and women in their
prime years for study and work. The main difference between the
present arrivals and those who came after the war, however, is that
nowadays most of them come alone. Almost a half of the households
in the Helsinki region in the 1990's have consisted of only one person,
a doubling of the figure over the last 25 years. This independence and
self-reliance is fostered by the fact that the region continues to have
a high proportion of small apartments, over half of them comprising
only one or two rooms. The renewed interest in living in the centre
has also increased the prestige of the old working-class districts such
as Punavuori, Kamppi, Kallio, Sörnäinen, Hermanni and Kumpula.

Helsinki has a long tradition of successful planning of its more
public central areas – and a long tradition of taking its time over com-
pleting the construction work. Particularly problematical has been the
"Terrace Square" at the entrance to the Kamppi area and the remaining area on the shore of Töölönlahti. These together form one of the
prime development sites in the city in terms of both location and status, bordered as they are by Parliament House, the Main Post Office
and the Railway Station. Helsinki is gradually finding itself faced with
the same situation as many other large European cities: that the functions necessary in a community are altering and institutions that re-
quire large amounts of space, such as factories, transport terminals,

hospitals, harbours, marshalling yards, schools and colleges, etc., are moving away, creating new opportunities for developing the functions that still belong to the city centre. The vacant area in Kamppi and Töölö has come about largely for reasons such as this. The area has for a long time been owned mainly by the state, but the railway goods yard and freight handling station is no longer needed close to the city centre, as these functions have been moved further out, partly to Pasila. The area released in this way would be ideal for public buildings of either national or municipal significance. In addition, traffic around Töölönlahti is still an important problem.

Repeated efforts have been made to devise plans for the Kamppi and Töölönlahti area since 1912, and the problem was approached with new enthusiasm after the war, when a proposal for a new town plan covering the central parts of Helsinki was put forward by Professor Yrjö Lindegren and the architect Erik Kråkström. The "most far-reaching solutions and planning programmes" in their proposal were connected with traffic arrangements, for which purpose a mighty express highway to the north was envisaged, with huge viaducts, intersections and tunnels.

Since it was still uncertain where the boundaries between state and city land ran, it was decided to commission the architect Professor Alvar Aalto to continue the work of planning the city centre. He submitted his plan in two stages, in 1961 and 1965, and the final decision on it was made by the City Council in 1966. The council greeted the plan and its architect with a standing ovation. One of Aalto's new ideas was to use Pasila as an extension to the business district of the city centre as well as Kamppi, and he also proposed a monumental open square in the Terrace Square area in front of Parliament House and the lining of the shore of Töölönlahti with buildings of cultural significance, partly on piles and landfill material.

Aalto's philosophy of urban architecture was that urbanism is based on a built environment; he found natural surroundings incongruous in a city. One remark of his stood out: "You will never succeed in turning Töölönlahti and the Hesperia Park into a miniature idyll. It would be nothing more than comical to place a copy or adaptation of a lake from the depths of the Karelian forest in the heart of a big city." Time passed by Aalto's ambitious plan, however. It did contain adjustments for vastly increased volumes of traffic, but his road system was regarded as too cumbersome, too expensive and impossible to implement. The only part of his plan that came to immediate fruition was the Finlandia Hall, completed in 1971. His proposal to build an opera house on the site of the old sugar refinery beside Töölön-

Many attempts have been made over the last 100 years or so to design a monumental centre for the Republic of Finland in the Töölönlahti area in front of Parliament House, and now, in the early years of the 21st century, all we can say is that the building work is still going on. The Finlandia Hall, designed by Alvar Aalto and completed in 1971, serves as the city's principal concert hall and conference centre and is one of its outstanding symbols.

lahti was not taken up until later. The new building was opened to the public in 1992.

Planning in Helsinki gained momentum in other ways, too, during the 1990s. The Kiasma Museum of Contemporary Art was opened in spring 1998, and the Cable Factory museum centre in 1999. Political developments and economic integration in Europe and internal migration within Finland meant that Helsinki began to perceive a new role for itself as a European metropolis and showcase for the Finnish economy on the world stage. The key words in this process were qualitative economic change and the creation of information networks and a network economy. The City Council began a programme of collaboration with the university and private companies, and the question of the restrictive nature of local authority boundaries and the need to form an integral metropolitan area became a more urgent one, remaining so ever since.

During the 1990s the city's international connections became a matter of principle on which its future was seen to rest. Globalization has raised it to the status of a powerful economic region within Northern Europe, and this has led to greater efforts to project its image, to provide its inhabitants with the everyday comforts of life and to improve standards of living, logistics, traffic conditions and the quality of the social surroundings. One European feature was the fact that culture was discovered as a strategy to be employed in this. Helsinki applied for and gained the status of one of the Cultural Capitals of Europe in the year 2000, and culture was combined with an attractive image and defined in a broad sense to include everything from design to ice hockey and from street cafés to after-dark art happenings.

Helsinki has been consciously planned during the last ten years to be a more densely constructed, urbanized community. The programme for filling in the gaps in the suburban structure has been supported by a determined effort to restore the city centre to the status that it deserves, which has been done by emphasizing its cultural stratification, its maritime character and its green spaces. Work was begun on renovating many of its historical buildings, while the outstanding new building project was the Kamppi complex, completed in 2005, at the same time as planning of the central area of Pasila began. The Central Bus Station at Kamppi was moved underground and a new shopping precinct was built on top of it. Work on the building of a new concert hall began in 2006, and new residential areas are

Kiasma, the Museum of Contemporary Art, housed in a building designed by the American architect Steven Holl, was opened to the Helsinki public in 1998.

Work on the building of the new Fishing Port residential area is due to begin some time after 2010. The actual harbour facilities will close down once Helsinki gains its modern large-scale port at Vuosaari. The urban employment and residential environment to be constructed there will take advantage of the proximity of the sea and the industrial and historical traditions attached to the area.

springing up in the city centre, at Jätkäsaari and Sörnäinen, around the fishing harbour and along the shore of the Arabia district. Traffic is being excluded from many of the streets in the centre, and the dream of a tunnel taking traffic under the central area is still very much alive. Helsinki can be expected to change much more quickly in the coming years than it has done for decades. The capital of Finland has a strong belief in its future!

LIFE, POLITICS AND IDEOLOGIES
IN THE METROPOLIS

It was on the eve of Independence Day 1948 that the Ministry of Supply gave permission for the lights to be switched on in the shop windows and neon signs of Helsinki for the first time since the war. The result was by no means a great blaze of urban splendour, as there were precisely three neon signs alight in Aleksanterinkatu, for instance, and in many other places only some of the letters in a sign could be made to work, but the lights did symbolize the expectations of better times to come. The reporter "Kati" in Helsingin Sanomat spoke of an awakening from seven years of slumber. Everyday life in Helsinki had been badly constricted by the war and the shortages of the reconstruction period, and the "card game" of rationing that affected almost all goods was to go on for some years yet, well into the early 1950's. The black market flourished and many Helsinki people were forced to admit how convenient it was to have country cousins. De-rationing of the last commodity, coffee, was announced in the winter of 1954, and it was in the same year that the last inhabitants of the Helsinki air-raid shelters were re-housed.

The political winds of change that the new age brought with it were felt most clearly of all in Helsinki. The restoration of the communists from their underground exile in 1945 increased the general political turbulence, and the streets and squares of the capital, particularly the Exhibition Hall and the area in front of Parliament House, became important arenas for the testing of the political strengths of the various factions. The communists' mass meetings, demonstrations and extraparliamentary activities lent much colour to the outdoor life of the city in the late 1940's, and before long ideological counter-activity became equally conspicuous. The war crimes tribunals of 1945–46 brought many people out onto the streets in protest, until eventually the wartime prime minister Edwin Linkomies and the foreign minister Väinö Tanner were released in 1948 and President Paasikivi announced a pardon for ex-President Ryti. The largest of all post-war demonstrations was organized by Helsinki University Students' Union in May 1948, when 8000 students assembled in the Senate Square and the Kumtähti sports ground to celebrate the centenary of the Finnish national anthem. The ideological content of the celebration was thus a commitment to national independence. On the other hand, the general strike of January 1956, which posed a serious threat to national unity, similarly began in the capital.

There were two major events in the post-war period that served to raise the spirits of the people of Helsinki in particular. The first of these was the city's 400th Anniversary, which was celebrated with lavish ceremony in June 1950. A foretaste of this was enjoyed in the late spring of the same year, in the form of a combined public degree ceremony for the Faculties of Philosophy and Social Sciences of the University of Helsinki, the first ceremony of its kind for 14 years. The 400th Anniversary itself was celebrated with the unveiling of a commemorative plaque in the Old Town and the opening of the new Gustav Vasa road. A historic parade took place through the city to the stadium, where a great celebration was held. Different parts of the city held their own local celebrations, too, and there were numerous exhibitions and lectures on the history of Helsinki. The city's own cultural aspirations were reflected in a Sibelius Week, arranged for the first time in 1951, a programme which later developed into the annual event known as the Helsinki Festival.

A much greater national effort was involved in the other highlight of the period, the Olympic Games of 1952. Preparations had originally been made to hold this great festival of sport in the city in 1940, but the war had intervened. The decision taken in 1947 to award the Olympics to Helsinki again was taken as a major act of recognition for Finland as a fully-fledged member of the international sports community. The games also left their permanent marks on the external appearance of the city, as the City Council took responsibility not only for traffic within the city and for policing and the maintenance of law and order, but also for the construction of the necessary venues for the games. The Olympic Stadium, the main arena for the event, had been built in 1938, and the work was continued in the late 1940's with the provision of a riding stadium at Ruskeasuo, a Swimming Stadium, a Sports Hall, a Velodrome and a Rowing Stadium. The Olympic village built at Koskela over the period 1940–1952 is regarded as the first example of a modern residential suburb in Finland.

The Olympic Games also inspired many other projects aimed at improving standards of city life and caused numerous public works schemes to be brought forward. The airfield at Seutula (later the Helsinki-Vantaa Airport) was taken into use just before the Olympics, water and electricity supplies, sewerage, street lighting and roads were improved, parks were refurbished, restaurant and hotel buildings were renovated, the funfair at Linnanmäki was built and improvements were made to the Korkeasaari Zoo. Many other build-

ings were also taken over for the duration of the games themselves: the Finnish athletes were housed in the cadet college at Santahamina, those from the eastern bloc countries were located in the newly completed halls of residence of the Technological University in Otaniemi, the women athletes were accommodated in the nursing school at Meilahti and the press were placed in the Student Union's Domus Academica and Satakunta House halls of residence.

The opening ceremony of the Olympic Games on 19th July 1952 was a stirring occasion in spite of the rain. The torch lit in Greece had been carried all through the country from Tornio to Helsinki and was borne into the Stadium itself by Finland's national Olympic hero Paavo Nurmi, who then lit the Olympic Flame. The games also transformed Helsinki into an international city, as products appeared in the shops that had only been dreamed about previously, including the most popular soft drink in the world, Coca-Cola. The event was looked back on nationally with a general sense of satisfaction and a unanimous feeling that the arrangements had worked smoothly and the spirit of the games had remained good throughout. Much appre-

One essential mark of spring in Helsinki is the succession of ceremonies which are held by the various faculties of the University of Helsinki at intervals of 3-5 years to confer master's and doctoral degrees. The photograph shows young graduates who have just received their master's degree in procession from the main building of the university to the Cathedral in May 1950.

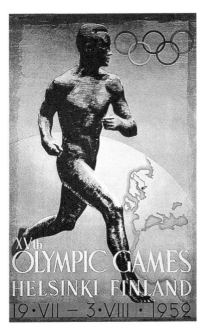

The Helsinki Olympic Games of 1952 were an important manifestation of national unity.

Emil Zatopek of Czechoslovakia, with his multiple gold medals, became the hero of the 1952 Olympic games in Helsinki. He is pictured here with Alain Mimoun of France, who won the silver medal in the 5000 metres, as they congratulate each other after the race. The Helsinki games has gained a reputation as "the last real sports event" before the commercialization of sport set in.

ciation was expressed of the Finns' hospitality, and it has often been claimed in later years that the Helsinki Games were "the last real Olympics" before commercialization took over.

Internationalism and modernism brought a breath of fresh air to the politics and ideologies of the capital in many other ways, too, during the 1950's, and as before, the demands for change spread like waves out into the remainder of the country in the course of time. The national identity continued for a long time after the war to be constructed in home-grown, agrarian terms, with the aim of maintaining a patriotic spirit and a sense of national unity. There was much ideological and political skirmishing, mainly in Helsinki cultural and university circles, over efforts to diversify the nation's cultural affiliations and create a more open-minded, pluralistic society. The chief protagonists were the urban reformers and the more conservative supporters of national tradition, with the former in the minority. The advocates of a patriotic and domestic cultural direction saw themselves as engaged in battle with the continentally oriented modernists, whom they regarded as being "lacking in ideals". By the 1960's this conflict had become a political one and began to affect the possibilities for achieving democracy, equality and welfare.

The initial forum for these debates was the cultural life of the capital and the structures that maintained this culture. There was a need "to find direction from visibility in an age that was somewhat turbid", as Eino S. Repo, one of the left-wing liberals among the reformers, put it. The revivalists of poetry, prose, the theatre and the cinema called for a more aesthetic, more international, more urbane and more individualistic approach to art. The development of interest in the cinema in the 1950's was a characteristically Helsinki-based phenomenon, the watching of artistic films, a pursuit which had taken root in pre-war days, having now become the prerogative of the city liberals.

The cinema played an important role in colouring the emotional experiences of young people in post-war times, and in shaping the emerging identity of the younger generation. The years of expansion of the cinema as a pastime in Helsinki occurred precisely in the early 1950's, prior to the spread of television on a national scale.

The battle over directions in culture was closely connected with the great transformation of Finnish society through urbanization and the emergence of the middle class, trends in which the Finland of the 1940's had lagged far behind the other western industrialized countries. The countryside was still the living environment with which the majority of Finns identified most readily, and as little study had been made of the history of the Finnish towns and their social conditions, people's assumptions regarding the contrasts between urban and rural environments were based on imagination, value judgements and prejudices. An opposition between "the good in the countryside" and "the evil in the town" was characteristic of the ideological and political climate at the time when migration to Helsinki began to increase sharply in volume.

Elsewhere in the country a great deal of suspicion was felt for Helsinki, the spirit that prevailed there and the tendency for the nation's affairs to be centred around the city. City life was looked on as spiritually debilitating and inclined to lead to indolence, ideological degeneration and foppery. People spoke of "betrayal by the intellectuals", of the tendency for the elite and well educated to remain in the Babel of Helsinki to pursue their careers, and expressed their disgust at the demise of the national academic tradition whereby those who had received an advanced education went out into the backwoods to encounter ordinary people. Urho Kekkonen, during his term as prime minister, was constantly drawing attention to the flight from the countryside and the problems that this entailed for the "asphalt peasants". Attempts were made by means of psychological investigations to demonstrate that town life led to the development of a human type that was incompatible with the Finnish character. There was a fear that Helsinki would serve as a channel for the spread of an "American business mentality" or a "Soviet party mentality" into Finland, as Dr. Matti Kuusi expressed it in a pamphlet on cultural policy in 1957.

The many novelties of the age reflected the growth in the numbers of young people and in their visibility within society and the general influence of popular culture. Finnish society became younger towards the late 1950's, as the children of the post-war boom reached consumer age. The adults were set talking by the flat caps, leather jackets, greased hair and the invasion of rock 'n roll. Young people's fashions had also achieved a breakthrough by the beginning of the next decade, and Beatles mania hit Helsinki in 1963, when the group visited Finland. A new, modern youth identity of American origin took shape in the towns first of all. It was not primarily a working-class phenomenon, however, as the most enthusiastic devotees of popular music were to be found in the middle-class homes. This was to be seen very clearly in Helsinki, as a university city, in that the dances and club nights held by the *nationes* attracted clientèle as never before.

Youth fashions required a forum of their own, of which the main exponent for a long time was the Teenage House in Kaisaniemi. Two

The student newspaper's interpretation of the dangers of the city in 1958.

of the main department stores in the city, Pukeva and Stockmann, also opened sections specifically aimed at young people, SevenTeens and Club 17. Since the main concentration of young people was in the suburbs, large numbers of youth clubs appeared at this time, the first being opened in Maunula in 1966. Meanwhile the coffee shops and refreshment bars of the city centre, such as those owned by Nissen, Stockmann, Colombia and Elanto, attracted the young people there. The first snack bar in Finland was opened in the Potato Square (later known as the Student Square) in 1959, and began marketing French fried potatoes, hamburgers and soft ice. Later it was the Esplanade Park and the Railway Station that began to win over the school-age clientèle, while the Expo Hall in the Barracks Square also became a popular meeting place for young people in the 1960's.

The decade of the 1950's and its ideals created the foundation for the later pattern of urban life. A new poetry of love and urbanism developed in the footsteps of Mika Waltari and Olavi Paavolainen, and novels and short stories considered people's relationships to the city and city life. Authors such as Kirsi Kunnas, Lassi Nummi, Anselm Hollo, Pentti Holappa, Jörn Donner, Anders Cleve, Eva Wichman, Arvo Turtiainen and Tuomas Anhava introduced new forms of urban description into literature. The slang spoken in the city finally became an object of serious research, so that it had achieved some sort of linguistic identity of its own, although not as exclusive as was maintained, in a slightly conceited manner, by the students' cultural jour-

Young people listening to the latest records in the music department of Stockmann in the 1950's. Pop music and the youth culture made its breakthrough in Finland around the same time as it did elsewhere in Europe.

nal *Eteläsuomalainen* in 1954: "But then, if you want to understand this language you must be born in Helsinki and have knocked about in as many of its backyards, basements and rocky parks as possible– –"

The ideological debate over the virtues of the towns and countryside, combined with national plans for developing Northern Finland, gave rise to a general policy of devolution and decentralization during the next decade. A need had been perceived after the war for a countrywide plan based on policies of "national reunification", and the reconstruction period had created favourable conditions for a transfer to long-term, centrally controlled economic, cultural and social planning. As the parties' began to complete their own cultural and regional policy statements by the mid-1960's, it was seen that an unusually great consensus of opinion existed in favour of regional development, the movement of government departments to other towns and cities and the founding of provincial universities. This meant that the focus of the national discussion on matters of development shifted away from the centres and the aim came to be the evening out of differences between the towns and the countryside.

The Helsinki-centred nature of legislation, administration, industry and economics became an object of harsh political scrutiny in the course of the 1960's. Demands were voiced for lessening the gap between the affluent south and the vast, impoverished hinterland. The point of departure was naturally the overwhelming position of Helsinki relative to the rest of the country and the proportions that migration to the capital had reached. Numerous parliamentary committees considered in their reports questions of the movement of offices and departments to other cities, and the devolution of government functions by strengthening the autonomy of the provincial and local authorities. It was believed that it would be possible in this way to create a number of strong, diversified growth centres to offset the power of the national capital. In the end, this was best achieved by the creation of a network of provincial universities and colleges.

The situation was a paradoxical one in many respects. The further urbanization proceeded, the more the multifarious problems suffered by the provinces captured the political limelight. Still more attention than ever was paid to the rural problems engendered by these rapid structural changes following the victory of the Agrarian Party in the elections of 1962, to the extent that the concentration of population in the metropolitan area and the emergence of urban planning may be said to have given rise to a tension of such proportions that its resolution has become one of the key issues in the politics of recent dec-

Young people began to make themselves seen and heard in quite a new fashion in the Helsinki of the 1950's. The "flat caps" in the picture were the identification mark of the first urban grouping of young people. The rise in standards of living was reflected in an increase in entertainments in the city and in an improvement in their quality. This comment by the cartoonist "Kari" is from 1952.

ades. The idea was even put forward in 1965 of transferring the capital "to somewhere in Central Finland, perhaps round about Jyväskylä", as the proposal framed by Jouko Loikkanen, secretary to Prime Minister Johannes Virolainen, read. The idea lived on for some years in administrative circles as work continued on preparing regional development legislation. The accumulation of academic functions in Helsinki continued to be a problem in the 1960's, as may be appreciated from the remark by *Provincia*, the young people's provincial and regional policy association, that "The capital is a swollen head that is poised to gobble up the whole of Uusimaa and would make Lahti into one of its suburbs tomorrow".

The structural change that was taking place nationally cleared the way for a new emphasis on ideology, so that the 1960's also witnessed the extensive awakening of an urban mentality. Again the stimuli for this came predominantly from academic circles in Helsinki. The values espoused by the younger generation set out from demands for individual freedom, psychological mobility, rationality, pluralist ethics, pacifism, internationalism and tolerance, all features of city life. These were aimed at breaking down the national tradition dating from the 19th century, the structures that belonged to the Finland of the estates, the uniform agrarian culture with its altruism and Christian concepts of morality and respectability. The New Left in the academic world levelled its criticism at the (bourgeois) values of home, church, school and army, a trend that became particularly poignant after the general election of 1966, in which the left wing gained a majority in parliament. The first modern urban "revolutionary show", which has since gained almost a mythical character, was the students' occupation of the Old Student House in November 1968.

The new realism in art, wild happenings in the towns and pop art rose to become the hallmarks of the modern trend in culture. The best-known literary wars were waged in Helsinki, and it was the people of Helsinki who queued for the ARS reviews of international modern art in 1961 and 1969. The 1960's were also the golden age of traditional monumental art. The statue of Mannerheim on horseback was unveiled with great ceremony in 1960, and soon afterwards came the series of statues of former presidents produced by Wäinö Aaltonen for sites outside Parliament House. The most ardent controversy arose over Eila Hiltunen's abstract monument to Sibelius, unveiled in 1967. All told, about twenty significant monuments were erected in the city in the space of a decade.

The radicalism of the 1960's was urban in character. The herald of this new direction in political thought, the Committee of Hundred,

which was opposed to the Arms Race, was originally a city move-ment, with its roots in the literary modernism, liberalism and cultural debates of the previous decade. One figurehead for all that was mod-ern and radical was the *Lapualaisooppera*, the "Opera to the Lapua Move-ment", composed by Kaj Chydenius to words by Arvo Salo, which was performed at the 40th Anniversary of the Student Theatre in 1966. Jazz, hootenanny, folk music and the first discotheques all came to the national consciousness as pursuits of the young people of Helsinki. One popular group, *Muksut*, "The Kids", performed the "I'll go wher-ever I'll go" songs and all-purpose lyrics in an urban vein written by Pentti Saarikoski and Anselm Hollo. Other poets who eulogised over Helsinki apart from Saarikoski and Salo were Pentti Saaritsa, Claes An-dersson and Viljo Kajava.

Post-war trends in the cinema point to a change in the emphasis placed on Helsinki. The attempts at depicting the town and country-side as opposites lent support to the traditional form of movie nar-

The student unrest of 1968 culminated in the students occupying their own building on the eve of the centenary of the Helsinki University Students' Union. The banner on the balcony of the Old Student House that reads "The university revolution has begun" links the occupation with the wave of student demonstrations experienced throughout the world at that time.

rative with its roots in the class society. The rapid changes had given rise to uncertainty, which placed the accent on the significance of old-standing values, roots and country idylls. The basic structure of a Finnish film was centred around a journey from the countryside into a town, and frequently also a return to the countryside. These works created and renewed stereotypic black-and-white pictures of the towns as dens of stress, crowds and sin, and Helsinki was described in the old Finnish films as a stage for upper class merrymaking, or else the harbours and backstreets of the capital might serve as the location for a crime film. It was only in the 1960's that a new wave began that altered entirely the manner in which people in Helsinki were portrayed. The characters of Chief Inspector Palmu and Maunu Kurkvaara created by Matti Kassila and Mika Waltari and the many films of Mikko Niskanen, Risto Jarva, Jaakko Pakkasvirta and Jörn Donner served to demonstrate that the city had become a normal place in which to live. The first suburban movie was Tapio Suominen's *Täältä tullaan, elämä!*, "Look out, life, here we come!" produced in 1980. The city environment, and that of Helsinki in particular, then gained a mythical dimension in the films of Aki Kaurismäki from the 1980's onwards.

The cheerful, urbane, pluralistic and affluent 1960's, ever eager to experiment and to play about with its new-found freedom, came to a full stop in Helsinki with the oil crisis of 1973 and the subsequent recession. The people of the city were encouraged to cut down on fuel consumption, and the public sector led the way by having the street lights of Helsinki functioning at half power and economising on the use of lighting for shop signs and advertisements. The change in mood was a very sudden one, on account of these economies and the concurrent tension in world politics. The rise in fuel prices and the increased unemployment that occurred around 1975 reduced the city dwellers' feeling of personal security. President Kekkonen himself declared a "state of national emergency", which indeed represented the true state of affairs. Economic indicators pointed downwards, inflation was on the rise, and the country's trade deficit was widening alarmingly. All this meant that Helsinki grew in importance as the main scene of party and trade union activity. Collective bargaining negotiations took place there, as did consultations over the forming of new governments, while the large-scale strikes and demonstrations of the 1970s were to be perceived in its streets and in the atmosphere conveyed by its media. And the focal point for the exercise of power was naturally President Kekkonen's official residence of Tamminiemi.

The rapid growth experienced in Helsinki in the 1960's created a good foundation for increases in the services provided by society, and it was during the following decade that a comprehensive network of day centres for children was created and work was undertaken to develop the care provided for the elderly. The task of arranging local authority health centres was commenced in 1972, and Helsinki went over to the comprehensive school system in 1977. Some light was made to shine in the darkness of world politics in 1975, when the third phase of the Conference on Security and Cooperation in Europe (CSCE), the ceremonial signing of the final document, was arranged in Helsinki. This established the "spirit of Helsinki" embodied in that document, a spirit of conciliation and impartiality, as a concept in international parlance and allowed the Finnish capital to serve, under the leadership of President Kekkonen, as the scene for an international political event at which the heads of the great powers of East and West sat around the same table. The CSCE and its follow-up organization were later to prove their worth when the countries of Eastern Europe began to sever their ties with communism in the late 1980's.

The achievement of a national programme for economic recovery in 1977 led to an improvement in the country's fortunes, the growth being based on intensive trade between Finland and the Soviet Union. The result was that the next decade was once more a time of high consumption, general affluence, the accumulation of wealth and the

Helsinki has played important roles in many modern movies. The director Aki Kaurismäki placed the main characters in Helsinki in many of his films produced in the 1980's, providing perceptive descriptions of parts of the city and its suburbs at different times of day and seasons of the year. Here we see the "trip to the country" in the film Ariel, one of Kaurismäki's "working class trilogy", which is set somewhere on the boundary between the town and the countryside.

"Lasipalatsi", the Glass Palace, a building that radiated light and urban frivolity, was the most modern concentration of shops, offices and entertainments in Helsinki in the 1930's. It was restored in the 1990's and still occupies an important position close to the new Kamppi precinct.

pursuit of material values, leading the media to conduct an analysis in the 1980's of the nature of the new narcissistic, individualist city culture. Helsinki gained numerous new shopping precincts, the opening gambit being the rebuilding of the Kaivopiha centre, followed soon afterwards by the East City complex, the Forum building, the new wing of the Stockmann department store and the Kluuvi Gallery. A number of multistorey carparks and underground walkways between stores in the city centre were built in the 1990's, and also the Kämp Gallery.

Leisuretime activities also thrived during this period. Fitness clubs and gymnasia were built in Helsinki and other cities, and holidays abroad gained in popularity. Time-share apartments came onto the market, as did subscriptions to golf clubs. And the epitome of this *nouveau riche* lifestyle was naturally to be found in Helsinki. The opening up of the financial markets raised the young, successful bankers, dealers, stock exchange speculators and large-scale investors with their newly acquired wealth to the status of symbols of their decade. Other manifestations of the new freedom were the numerous local radio stations and a new generation of magazines. A few of the newcomers among these, such as *Image* and *City magazine*, proved reasonably durable. The new trends also meant that the metropolitan region became a powerful magnet for concentrations of the new media, PR operations and information technology companies.

On the other hand, Helsinki was hit by the severe recession of the early 1990's in the same way as the rest of the country. The collapse of trade with Russia led to widespread bankruptcies in the clothing, shipbuilding and metalworking industries, and the aftermath of the casino economy proved the downfall of some banks. The economic recession and the rapid rise in unemployment brought queues for free food parcels to the Helsinki street scene. The crisis of the welfare state forced both the public and the private sector to cut costs and reduce wage bills. A mood of depression was clearly in evidence, with inequality and alienation becoming accentuated in some areas. At the same time the city was having to adapt to a multicultural situation and respond to the challenge presented by an influx of refugees, asylum seekers and immigrants.

Some hope for the future was raised by the decision to join the European Union, which was celebrated in earnest in Helsinki in October 1994. Optimism for the future was also kindled in the latter half of the decade by the choice of Helsinki as one of the Cultural Capitals of Europe for the year 2000. Culture was also brought to the fore through the creation of a number of multipurpose centres for the arts, the cinema and museums in old vacated properties throughout the city: the Glass Palace, Nokia's former Cable Factory, the tram depot in Mannerheimintie and the forer Tennis Hall, all of which were given an urbane, cultural face-lift. Also, in the wake of the sports boom of the 1990s, a decision was taken to build the most modern multipurpose sports and entertainments hall in Europe, the Hartwall Arena, and the determination to "put Helsinki on the map" was again in evidence in 2007 when the European Song Contest was held in Finland for the first time in this same hall.

The internal migration of population has brought more and more of the Finns within the scope of urban life and the life of the metropolis, and much deliberation continues to take place over the nature of urbanism in Finland, the urban way of life, habits and customs and what it means to live in Helsinki. One thing, at least, is certain: Helsinki remains a melting pot in this respect, a forerunner and model for the whole country, arousing both admiration and hostility among people in other parts of the country.

MILESTONES IN THE LIFE OF THE CAPITAL

Helsinki became the capital of Finland in all respects during the last decades of the Grand Duchy period. In addition to its central government institutions, it possessed the only university in the country, a university of technology and other forms of higher education and the main offices of practically all the nationwide societies and associations. The same was true of the political parties, trade unions, the large commercial banks (with the exception of *Pohjoispankki*, the "Northern Bank", which was based in Vyborg) and the main insurance companies. Although most industrial companies had their registered offices at their factory sites, the joint export organizations for the pulp, paper and fibre board industries were in Helsinki. The other notable Finnish towns, Turku, Vyborg and Tampere, were very much smaller, and although St. Petersburg exercised a great attraction and considerable numbers of Finns lived there, Finland was organized as an entity of its own in virtually all spheres of life.

The dawn of the new republic speeded up this centralization and made it more essential than ever, especially when the boundary with Russia, which had previously been little more than a formality, was closed almost entirely in 1918 and the situation finalized under the Peace of Tartu in 1920. Even tourist journeys between Finland and the Soviet Union became possible only in 1956, and customs and immigration control has been very strict on both sides of the border. The need for this has been confirmed in recent times with Finland's new status as a member of the European Union from 1995 onwards and a signatory to the Schengen Agreement. These controls have not prevented the passage of goods, however, which at some stages has reached quite substantial proportions. There are borders with Sweden and Norway in Lapland which are easy to cross, but otherwise Finland has been virtually an island since 1918.

The loss of Karelia to the Soviet Union in 1940, and finally in 1944, brought new population to Helsinki, and also new customs associated with life in Vyborg.

The independent state of Finland gained its own president in 1919, with the former Imperial Palace as his official residence. This arrangement was altered in 1994, when the president and his wife moved to the new, modernistic residence of Mäntyniemi in the Meilahti area of

In all its external simplicity, the Presidential Palace, formerly the Imperial Palace, beside the Market Square, is a powerful symbol of Finland's role as an independent state. Ceremonial state visits formed an important element in Finnish foreign policy from the 1950's onwards up to the time of joining the European Union, as they enabled this small country located in an inconvenient geographical position to gain a great deal of international publicity and appreciation. The reception organized by the President on 6th December each year to mark Independence Day always arouses considerable interest.

the city, the Presidential Palace as such continuing to function largely in a ceremonial role.

Once Finland was independent, it gained its own *corps diplomatique* of accredited representatives of foreign states. Finland's active participation in the League of Nations and later in other international organizations, together with its interesting geopolitical location, has ensured that the body of foreign diplomats has been relatively large and active for a country of this size. In earlier times governments had consulates in Helsinki which were subordinate to their embassies in St. Petersburg. The 1975 CSCE conference, with its preparatory stages, and the Finnish presidency of the European Union in 1999 are examples of periods when other nations have seen fit to strengthen their representation, while there have also been stages when connections between East and West have been managed through foreign observers

147

The state visit was developed to perfection as an instrument of foreign policy by President Urho Kekkonen, a statesman whose character represented a blend of the dynamism of a sportsman, the intellect of an academic and the determination of a patriot. Here he is seen in top hat and tails, with his gloves in his hand, leading Marshal Voroshilov, President of the Soviet Union, out of the former imperial waiting room of the Railway Station in front of the crowds of onlookers.

in Helsinki. The presence of the diplomatic corps has had a profound effect on the nature of the city as a national capital since the 1920's.

On Independence Day, 6th December, the President of Finland and his wife hold a large reception in the Presidential Palace which still follows the etiquette of the Grand Duchy era, in which dancing, the wearing of medals and the splendid dresses of the ladies play a prominent part. The *corps diplomatique* and members of the Finnish parliament are among those invited, along with administrators, intellectuals and other outstanding personalities in society.

State visits also form an important part of official international contacts. These took place mainly with neighbouring countries in the early days. The first event of this kind, the visit by King Gustav V and Queen Victoria of Sweden, introduced the people of Helsinki to this ceremonial world, in the spirit of the visits made by the Tsars in the days of the Grand Duchy. After a long pause, King Gustav VI Adolf and Queen Louise of Sweden, with a naval escort, arrived in 1952, but it was only in the times of President Kekkonen in 1956–1981, that these visits became frequent events. Kekkonen took full advantage of such occasions to show outsiders the progress that had been made in Finland and to rectify misunderstandings, since the position of the president as both a ceremonial and a political figurehead allows the splendour of a state visit to be combined with political discussions. The hospitality shown in Finland then led to invitations to make impressive visits to other countries. Probably more state visits have been made to Finland than to any other comparable country.

The great socioeconomic expansion of the 1960's led to growth both in central and local government administration and in the private sector. This was to be seen in the ministries and the larger banks in particular.

It was possible for a long time to house all the government ministries in the former Imperial Senate building, to which extensions were added, but premises were later found for many of them elsewhere. The most impressive of all is the former barracks of the Finnish Marine Equipage, designed by Engel, on the peninsula of Katajanokka, which was restored and extended in the 1980's to provide a magnificent building for the Ministry of Foreign Affairs.

Finland traditionally had two large commercial banks, *Pohjoismainen Yhdyspankki*, the Nordic Union Bank, which originally had liberal affiliations, and *Kansallis-Osake-Pankki*, founded by the Fennomans. Each of these had absorbed a large number of smaller banks in the course of its existence, the last major takeover by the former having been that of *Helsingin-Osake-Pankki*, which in common with its two larger counterparts and the central clearing bank of the Savings Bank group, had its head office on Aleksanterinkatu. All these banks had networks of branch offices covering the whole country and close connections with the principal actors in the insurance and industrial sectors. The economic recession and bank crisis of the early 1990's nevertheless led to a complete reorganization of the Aleksanterinkatu banking world, in which the old rivals *Yhdyspankki* and

Kansallispankki were merged to form the *Merita* group in 1995 and this in turn merged with the Swedish *Nordbanken* in 1998. The latter half of the decade saw in fact very many mergers between large Finnish firms and Swedish counterparts, and to a great extent the head offices of the new organizations have remained in Helsinki.

The great upheavals in European history of the early 1990's took place very close to Finland and to Helsinki: in Russia, Germany, the Baltic States and Poland. The Soviet socio-political system was turned upside down remarkably suddenly, and the resulting federation then dispersed into numerous independent states. Estonia, Latvia and Lithuania broke away from Russia, the whole basis of society in Poland was renewed and the GDR was reunited with Federal Germany, but Russia remained as Finland's neighbour in the east and St. Petersburg continued to be the largest city on the Baltic Sea. The sphere of the Gulf of Finland is still one of frontiers and one of uncertainty, although trade and human contacts are increasing all the time and have altered the whole aspect of the region.

The reunification of Germany caused the European Community to become the European Union from 1993 onwards, and Finland and Sweden joined this union just over a year later, in January 1995. Estonia and Poland were in the first group of candidates for membership. The monetary and economic union stage in the history of the EU began in January 1999. Finland assumed the presidency for the EU for the first time in the latter half of the same year and for the second time in the latter half of the year 2006.

Helsinki still occupies a crucial socio-political position in the world, and it has grown in both political and cultural importance in the course of the 1990's. We are very well aware, however, that there is no escaping from the great forces and turning points of history. Instead, we must adopt an active attitude towards these in order to promote the values and aspirations that are most dear to us.

A LOOK INTO THE FUTURE

With the dawn of the new millennium the building of Helsinki entered a fresh dynamic phase. On the one hand work began on reshaping the large area of land in front of Parliament House that had once been the railway goods yard to create a park and on the building of a new Music Centre with concert halls and teaching premises on the western edge of this area, and on the other hand the block occupied by the Central Bus Station not far away from this was developed into the new Kamppi shopping and residential precinct with a modern, efficient Bus Station in its basement. This former parade ground for the Turku Barracks had been put to rather second-rate used for decades, and now, contrary to the situation in many other cities where bus traffic has been pushed further and further out towards the periphery, a new Bus Station has been provided at what is logistically the very heart of Helsinki, with direct connections to the Metro and the tram network and almost adjacent to the Railway Station. Another essential element in this new functional environment is the very lively centre for cultural activities created out of the former Tennis Hall, a complex of cinemas combined with extensive exhibition spaces for the City Art Museum. The building became extremely popular as soon as it was opened in 1999. Also very close at hand are the Zoological Museum, the National Museum, Helsinki City Museum in the Hakasalmi Villa and the Kiasma Museum of Contemporary Art, nor is the Atheneum Museum of Classical Finnish Art more than a few hundred metres away.

Work on another enormous project with far-ranging implications, the future commercial port at Vuosaari, finally began in 2003 after many rounds of planning and objections, and a new rail connection was laid out for it via the north of the city, partly through a long tunnel in order to preserve an area of forest and a nature reserve. When the port is opened in 2008 it will have the effect of releasing many existing harbours in Helsinki for other uses, one of which will be the projected residential area of Jätkäsaari, close to the existing modern housing and Metro station at Ruoholahti, and the maritime residential zone to be built at Munkkisaari and Hernesaari to the east of the city centre. Another large area of housing that is already under development in that part of the city comprises the environs of Vanhankaupunginlahti, the "Old City Bay", and the area beneath and on both sides of the Kulosaari bridge. This area of Sörnäinen and Hermannin-

The Kamppi precinct was completed in two phases. About a fifth of the building volume, including the long-distance bus terminal and some of the shops and cafés, was taken into use in summer 2005, and the 5-storey shopping centre above the terminal was officially opened on 2nd March 2006, by which time the apartments in the same complex were also ready for occupation. In the foreground is the old bus station, the former Turku Barracks.

ranta will merge with the existing residential and university suburb of Arabia, which has continued to develop during the present decade. The Arabia area and the adjacent suburb of Kumpula already house the Faculty of Science and part of the Faculty of Biosciences belonging to the University of Helsinki, also the University of Art and Design, Helsinki, and the Arcada Polytechnic. A further consequence of the completion of the port facilities at Vuosaari will be that the railway marshalling yard at Pasila serving the existing harbours in Helsinki will become redundant an the area will be available for the planned new Central Pasila development.

A third major project on the drawing board at the time of writing involves plans for the incorporation of parts of the neighbouring municipality of Sipoo, which has so far remained fairly rural in character, within the city boundaries. The city already owns large tracts of Sipoo, but these are mostly extensive areas of protected forest and cannot in themselves satisfy the city's need for additional building land further out from the East City Centre. In any case, the planning responsibility for these areas rests with Sipoo Municipal Council, which is reluctant to take the initiative in such matters.

DATES IN THE HISTORY OF HELSINKI

1550	Helsinki founded on the shores of the parish of Helsinge
1555	Helsinki used by King Gustavus Vasa as a base for the war against Russia The king visits the town
1569	Granting of the first rights and privileges of a town
1570	Destroyed by fire as the result of a Russian attack Also hit by an outbreak of plague
1616	Local assembly Visit by King Gustavus II Adolf
1640	Helsinki moved to its present site
1654	Two thirds of the town destroyed by fire
1695–1697	Years of severe famine
1713	The town is invaded by the Russians and razed to the ground
1727	Building of the Ulrika Eleonora Church
1748	Commencement of the building of Sveaborg
1808	The town is again invaded by the Russians and is destroyed by fire
1809	Two visits by Emperor Alexander I
1810	Appointment of a committee to supervise the rebuilding of the city
1812	Helsinki chosen by Alexander I to be the capital of Finland
1815	Town plan drawn up by J. A. Ehrenström
1816	C. L. Engel appointed architect in charge of construction work in the city
1820	Work begins on building the Naval Barracks Completion of the private house of Commercial Counsellor Heidenstrauch, which later became the Presidential Palace

1822	First phase of the Senate building taken into use
	Completion of the main building of the Guards Barracks
1827	First theatre building completed
1828	University moved from Turku to Helsinki
1829	Publication of the first real newspapers
1831	Founding of the Finnish Literature Society
1832	Completion of the main building of the University
1833	Visit of Emperor Nikolai I and Empress Alexandra
	Opening of the Seurahuone hotel
1837	Commencement of regular steamship services between
	Helsinki and St. Petersburg
1838	Kaivopuisto Spa opened to the public
1843	Opening of the Helsinki Observatory
1844	Completion of the University Library building
1845	Founding of the Symphonic Society
	The first art exhibition held in Helsinki
1852	Consecration of the Cathedral Church of St. Nicholas
	Performance of the first Finnish opera, with an
	all-Finnish cast
1855	Fortress of Sveaborg bombarded by the British and
	French navies
1860	Completion of the new theatre building
	(now the Swedish Theatre)
1862	Inauguration of the Helsinki–Hämeenlinna railway line
1863	Commencement of regular sessions of the Diet in
	Helsinki
1868	Building of the Uspensky Cathedral
1870	Opening of the Old Student House
	Opening of the Helsinki–St. Petersburg railway line
1875	First meeting of Helsinki City Council
1876	Finland's first industrial exhibition held in Helsinki
	Visit by Emperor Alexander II

1877	Premises of the Polytechnic College completed
1881	Opening of the Rikhardinkatu public library, the first of its kind in Helsinki
1884	Helsinki Workers' Association formed
1880's	Building of the Bank of Finland, State Archives and House of the Estates
1887	Opening of Hotel Kämp Northern Esplanade gains its present appearance
1888	Commencement of public transport by horsedrawn omnibus
1889	Atheneum building completed Opening of the Old Market Hall, the first of its kind in Finland
1902	Completion of the National Theatre building
1905	General strike
1906	Mutiny in the Sveaborg garrison
1906–1908	Work begins on building the first garden suburbs
1908	Building of the National Museum, the House of the Workers and the Kallio Church
1914	Suomenlinna (Sveaborg) becomes a significant naval base on the outbreak of the Great War
1914–1918	Building and inauguration of the new Railway Station
1915	Emperor Nikolai II makes what is to be his last visit to Helsinki
1917	Parliament approves the declaration of Finnish independence
1918	Helsinki taken over by the troops of the Whites Departure of the Russian warships
1920	First trade fair in Finland to be organized in Helsinki
1924	Air services to Tallinn and Stockholm inaugurated
1930	Opening of the new Stockmann department store
1931	Completion of Parliament House

1930's	Commencement of work on building Helsinki University Hospital
1939–44	Helsinki bombed on numerous occasions
1940	Inauguration of the sports arena later to become the Olympic Stadium
1946	Incorporation of neighbouring districts into the city Recognition of the division into city centre and suburbs
1950	400th Anniversary celebrations
1952	Olympic Games held in Helsinki Opening of the airfield at Seutula, later to become the Helsinki–Vantaa Airport
1950's	Building of Tapiola Garden Suburb Areas of suburban apartment blocks springing up on the outskirts of the city Increasing demolition of old buildings in the city centre
1962	Communist-inspired International Youth Festival held in Helsinki
1965	Alvar Aalto reveals his plan for developing the city centre Population of Helsinki exceeds half a million
1965–1970	More vehement discussions over the destruction of old buildings
1967	Helsinki City Theatre opened
1969	Completion of the Church in the Rock
1971	Finlandia Hall opened
1970's	Helsinki becomes a venue for the SALT disarmament negotiations
1975	Signing of the final document of the CSCE conference in Helsinki
1982	Opening of the first Metro line
1980's	Opening of the Kaivopiha and Forum shopping precincts
1992	Finnish State Opera moves to the new Opera House

1998	Opening of Kiasma (Chiasma), the Museum of Contemporary Art
1999	Completion of the new head offices of Sanoma Oy
2000	Helsinki is one of the Cultural Capitals of Europe and celebrates its 450th Anniversary
2005	Completion of the annex to Parliament House
2006	Opening of the new Bus Station and shopping precinct at Kamppi
2008	Completion of the port of Vuosaari
2009	Completion of the Helsinki Music Centre at Töölönlahti

ILLUSTRATIONS FROM

Otava Publishing Company's archives

EXCEPT FOR:
City Planning Department / Adactive Ltd., p. 130
Finnish Architectural Museum, p. 109, 144
Finnish Defence Forces, picture archives, p. 91, 99 (above)
Finnish Hotel and Restaurant Museum, p. 99
Finnish Press Agency, p. 102, 134 (below)/ Keystone, 147 /
   Hannu Männynoksa
Helsinki City Museum, historical picture archives, pp. 19, 49, 53,
   68 / Signe Brander, 70, 85, 112, 113, 112 113, 118 (above)
Helsinki City Transport p. 121 / Julia Lila
Helsinki University Museum, picture archives, pp. 23, 133
Matti Klinge, pp. 11, 14–15, 17 (top left), 21, 30, 38, 43, 45, 73, 90
Laura Kolbe, pp. 78, 82, 116, 118, 137
Lehtikuva, pp. 60 / Heikki Saukkomaa, 141, 152 / Kimmo Mäntylä
Lentokuva Vallas Oy, p. 128
Mannerheim Museum, picture archives, pp. 95, 96
Museum of Contemporary Art Kiasma, p. 129
Sputnik Ltd., / Marja-Leena Hukkanen, p. 143
Kari Suomalainen, p. 139